Natal'ia Vorozhbit

THE GRAIN STORE

translated by

SASHA DUGDALE

NICK HERN BOOKS

London

www.nickhernbooks.co.uk

ROYAL
SHAKESPEARE
COMPANY

ABOUT THE ROYAL SHAKESPEARE COMPANY

The Royal Shakespeare Company at Stratford-upon-Avon was formed in 1960 as a home for Shakespeare's plays, classics and new plays.

The first Artistic Director Peter Hall created an ensemble theatre company of mostly young actors and writers. The core of the work was Shakespeare, combined with a search for writers who were as true to their time as Shakespeare was to his. The Company was led by Hall, Peter Brook and Michel Saint-Denis. Hall's founding principles were threefold. He wanted the Company to embrace the freedom and power of Shakespeare's work, to train and develop young actors and directors and to experiment in new ways of making theatre. Rejecting dogma, he urged the Company in a 1963 address to "Keep open, keep critical... Our Company is young, we are searching, and whatever we find today, a new search will be necessary tomorrow."

The Company has had a distinct personality from the beginning. The search for new forms of writing and directing was led by Peter Brook. He pushed writers to experiment. "Just as Picasso set out to capture a larger slice of the truth by painting a face with several eyes and noses, Shakespeare, knowing that man is living his everyday life and at the same time is living intensely in the invisible world of his thoughts and feelings, developed a method through which we can see at one and the same time the look on a man's face and the vibrations of his brain."

A rich and varied range of writers flowed into the Company and have continued to do so with the RSC's renewed commitment to placing living dramatists at the heart of the Company. These include: Harold Pinter, Howard Barker, Edward Bond, Howard Brenton, Edward Albee, David Edgar, Peter Flannery, Martin Crimp, Caryl Churchill, Tony Harrison, Wole Soyinka, Stephen Poliakoff, Tom Stoppard, Timberlake Wertenbaker, Martin McDonagh, Marina Carr, debbie tucker green, David Greig, Rona Munro, Adriano Shaplin, Roy Williams and Anthony Neilson.

Alongside the Royal Shakespeare Theatre, The Other Place was established in 1975. The 400-seat Swan Theatre was added in 1986. The RSC's spaces have seen some of the most epic, challenging and era-defining theatre – Peter Brook's Beckettian *King Lear* with Paul Scofield in the title role, Charles Marowitz's *Theatre of Cruelty* season which premiered Peter Weiss' *Marat/Sade*, Trevor Nunn's studio *Macbeth*, Michael Boyd's restoration of ensemble with *The Histories Cycle* and David Greig's and Roy Williams' searing war plays *The American Pilot* and *Days of Significance*.

The Company today is led by Michael Boyd, who is taking the Company's founding ideals forward. His belief in ensemble theatre making, internationalism, in new work and active approaches to Shakespeare in the classroom has inspired the Company to landmark projects such as *The Complete Works Festival, Stand up for Shakespeare* and *The Histories Cycle*. He is overseeing the transformation of our theatres which will welcome the world's theatre artists onto our stages to celebrate the power and freedom of Shakespeare's work and the wealth of inspiration it offers to living playwrights.

The Grain Store is generously supported by
THE COLUMBIA FOUNDATION FUND OF THE CAPITAL COMMUNITY FUND

The RSC Ensemble is generously supported by
THE GATSBY CHARITABLE FOUNDATION and THE KOVNER FOUNDATION

The RSC Literary Department is generously supported by THE DRUE HEINZ TRUST

The RSC's New Work is generously supported by
CHRISTOPHER SETON ABELE on behalf of THE ARGOSY FOUNDATION

The RSC is grateful for the significant support of its principal funder,
Arts Council England, without which our work would not be possible.
Around 50 per cent of the RSC's income is self-generated from Box Office sales,
sponsorship, donations, enterprise and partnerships with other organisations.

REVOLUTIONS

This August, the RSC launched a four year celebration and exploration of theatre in Russia and the former Soviet Union. We begin with the première of two new RSC commissioned plays from Russia and Ukraine, performed by the RSC Ensemble. *The Grain Store* by Natal'ia Vorozhbit and *The Drunks* by Mikhail and Vyacheslav Durnenkov capture the voices of an exciting new generation of post-Soviet playwrights. *Revolutions* will culminate in a major Russian contribution to our 2012 Olympic celebration.

For over a century, Russian theatre has had a profound influence on theatre in the West and particularly that of the RSC. After Shakespeare, Chekhov is the most performed playwright in the world and Russian work has always featured heavily in the RSC's repertoire. Stanislavski began and is still at the heart of Western film and theatre practice. The RSC has broken free of this by also embracing the bold, expressive style championed by Stanislavski's rebellious pupil, Meyerhold, especially in Peter Brook's *A Midsummer Night's Dream*, Trevor Nunn's *Nicholas Nickleby* and Michael Boyd's *The Histories*.

We open *Revolutions* with our new plays. These plays are the first fruits of an adventure which began back in 2005. We are proud to be working with Associate Director International at the Royal Court, Elyse Dodgson, who was invited to join the RSC as consultant by our then Associate Director, Dominic Cooke. Dominic, Elyse and RSC Company Dramaturg Jeanie O'Hare went to Moscow to work with nine writers selected by Elyse from the emerging writers of Russia and Ukraine. Giving them stimuli from the classics while encouraging them to engage with contemporary Russian society, we gave the writers seed commissions. Of those nine, three were strong enough to become full commissions and two are now on our main stage. This development of international work is central to Michael Boyd's vision at the RSC and further projects are planned. We are delighted that in this case the searching intelligence of the Royal Court's international programme has been the key to unlocking a generation of writers who are hungry to write for large stages.

FROM COLLECTIVISATION TO
THE UKRAINIAN HOLODOMOR, 1928-1933
A TIMELINE

JANUARY – JUNE, 1928

In order to finance industrialisation, Stalin orders the seizing of wheat and other reserves for export using any means necessary. The peasants object fiercely.

SUMMER AND AUTUMN, 1928

Mikhail Bukharin suggests more moderate approaches to acquiring stock, and the extreme methods are discontinued. Yet after the Summer the violent requisitions begin again.

JANUARY – JUNE, 1929

Stalin launches the first of his Five-Year Plans, and begins to pursue ideas of collectivisation, in which several smaller farms are run as a joint enterprise. Resistance to this continues to grow, with around 1,300 peasant disturbances in the USSR.

JANUARY – JUNE, 1930

The instigation of collectivisation is preceded by the mass removal of skilled farmers (called *kulaks*) to distant collective farms. Between 1930 and 1931, 1.8 million people are deported. In Ukraine over a million peasants participate in revolts, leading Stalin to temporarily allow them to leave the collective farms. At the same time he orders a mass arrest of the Ukrainian intelligentsia.

SUMMER AND AUTUMN, 1930

An economic crisis ensues and wages are cut to half of what they had been in 1927. However, the crop is strong, and, thinking the battle won, Stalin mounts a new, ambitious industrial effort.

WINTER, 1930-31

The collective farm system is enforced again in a new wave of requisitions and deportations. The peasants call it a 'second serfdom'.

SUMMER AND AUTUMN, 1931

A mediocre crop yield is quickly requisitioned by a hungry army and a restless working class. Much is also exported to raise funds for technology, machinery, and to pay off German loans. Stalin's supporters in Ukraine express their concern. Kazakh nomads whose livestock have been requisitioned begin to die of mass hunger and disease.

SPRING, 1932

Ukrainian officials note the spreading of hunger and a large rural exodus. Local communists urge Stalin to reduce procurements, but the response is insufficient.

SUMMER, 1932

The Ukrainian Party registers its opposition to Stalin's policies, which he interprets as an alliance with the peasantry. He writes that the risk of 'losing Ukraine' is real.

AUTUMN, 1932

The crop is poor, and a combination of Stalin's policies, including those designed to exert control over the Republics and to tame the peasantry, leads to famine. Special forces are dispatched to 'redress the situation'. Those who have helped starving families are arrested or shot and all food reserves are requisitioned.

WINTER, 1932-33

In December two key policies are revoked – one which promoted the rights of local nationalities, including Ukrainians, and the promotion of Ukrainian culture in Russia is discouraged. In January Stalin orders political police to stop the exodus of peasantry from Ukraine.

FEBRUARY – JUNE, 1933

The greatest number of famine victims yet is recorded in Spring 1933. There are thought to be between 6 and 7 million victims of the *holodomor*, as it came to be known, spread primarily over Ukraine, Kazakhstan and the Northern Caucuses. It is believed that between 3.5 and 3.8 million people died from hunger and disease in Ukraine.

Debate continues about the causes of this mass famine, and records by the NKVD (and later KGB) were slowly opened. However, in 2008, the European Parliament legally declared it a 'crime against humanity'.

Based on an article by Andrea Graziosi, Professor of History at the University of Naples 'Federico II'.

This production of *The Grain Store* was first performed by the Royal Shakespeare Company at The Courtyard Theatre, Stratford-upon-Avon, on 10 September 2009. The cast was as follows:

YURKO, AN ACTOR	**Joseph Arkley**
OLYANA	**Noma Dumezweni**
LANDOWNER	**Geoffrey Freshwater**
MASHA, AN ACTOR	**Mariah Gale**
LIONECHKA/TODOS/GUARD	**Gruffudd Glyn**
TRAMP	**Greg Hicks**
GAVRILO	**Kathryn Hunter**
ARSEI'S MOTHER	**Kelly Hunter**
VASILII, AN ACTOR	**Ansu Kabia**
ARSEI PECHORITSA	**Tunji Kasim**
GAFIIKA/LIONECHKA'S MOTHER	**Debbie Korley**
MORTKO	**John Mackay**
SAMSON	**Forbes Masson**
ONIS'KO	**Dharmesh Patel**
ARTIUKH THE BURIER/ OLD WOMAN DANCING	**Patrick Romer**
YUKHIM	**David Rubin**
GOROBETS	**Oliver Ryan**
MOKRINA'S SISTER/NURSE	**Simone Saunders**
OLD WOMAN WITH AN EMPTY BUCKET	**Peter Shorey**
SAMOILENKA	**Katy Stephens**
IVAN IVANOVICH, AN ACTOR	**Sam Troughton**
RUDENKO, THE EDUCATOR	**James Tucker**
FEODOSII/GUARD	**Larrington Walker**
KILINA	**Kirsty Woodward**
MOKRINA STARITSKAYA	**Samantha Young**

All other parts played by members of the company.

Directed by	**Michael Boyd**
Designed by	**Tom Piper**
Lighting designed by	**Oliver Fenwick**
Music by	**John Woolf**
Sound designed by	**Nick Powell**
Movement by	**Anna Morrissey**
Company Dramaturg	**Jeanie O'Hare**
Company text and voice work by	**Alison Bomber and Tess Dignan**
Fights by	**Terry King**
Assistant Director	**Vik Sivalingam**
Music Director	**John Woolf**
Casting by	**Hannah Miller** CDG
Production Manager	**Mark Graham**
Costume Supervisor	**Poppy Hall**
Assistant Costume Supervisor	**Gayle Woodsend**
Company Manager	**Michael Dembowicz**
Stage Manager	**Robbie Cullen**
Deputy Stage Manager	**Alison Daniels**
Assistant Stage Manager	**Joanna Vimpany**

MUSICIANS

Guitars/Contrabass Balalaika	**Nicholas Lee**
Flute	**Ian Reynolds**
Clarinet	**Adam Cross**
Violin	**Ivor McGregor**
Accordion	**Karen Street/John Woolf**
Trombone	**Kevin Pitt**
Percussion	**James Jones**

The performance is approximately 2 hours and 45 minutes in length,
including one interval of 20 minutes.

EMBEDDED WRITERS AT THE RSC

The potential for new work at the RSC is something we take very seriously. Our embedded writer policy is just one of a raft of strategies designed to inspire playwrights.

We believe that a writer embedded with our actors helps establish a creative culture within the Company which both inspires new work and creates an ever more urgent sense of enquiry into the classics. The benefits work both ways. Actors naturally learn the language of dramaturgical intervention and sharpen their interpretation of roles. Writers benefit from re-discovering the stagecraft and theatre skills that have been lost over time. They regain the knack of writing roles for leading actors. They become hungry to put death, beauty and metaphor back on stage.

As part of this strategy we have played host to key international writers for the last three years. Tarell McCraney is our current RSC/CAPITAL Centre International Playwright in Residence. He works in the rehearsal room with the Ensemble Company on our Shakespeare productions. Whilst contributing creatively to the work of the directors and actors he is also developing his own writing and theatre practice. His new play for the RSC will be performed by this current Ensemble in 2011. His post is funded by the CAPITAL Centre at Warwick University where he teaches as part of his residency.

Tarell follows on from Adriano Shaplin who was with the RSC from 2006-8.

We also invite British writers to spend time with us in the rehearsal room and contribute dramaturgically to both our main stage Shakespeares and our Young People's Shakespeare. There is a generation of playwrights who are ready to write their career-defining work. We are creating conditions at the heart of the RSC in which this generation can take themselves seriously as dramatists and thrive.

Special thanks go to Elyse Dodgson, Dominic Cooke, Rachael Barber, Ludmila Anestiadi, and everyone who helped with our Moscow workshops; Tanya Oskolkova, Vladimir Fleisher, Igor Troilin and all the staff at Meyerhold Theatre Center; Elena Kovalskaya at Lubimovka Young Playwrights Festival; and Elena Gremina at Theatre.Doc.

THE COMPANY

JOSEPH ARKLEY

YURKO, AN ACTOR
RSC DEBUT SEASON:
Archidamus/Officer
in *The Winter's Tale*,
Remus/Octavius Caesar/
Artemidorus in *Julius
Caesar*, Yurko, an Actor in
The Grain Store.
understudy: Vasilii, an
Actor.
trained: Royal Scottish
Academy of Music and
Drama (winner of the 2006
Laurence Olivier bursary).
theatre includes: *Moonlight*
(Arches Theatre); *Cotton
Wool* (Theatre503); *The Glass
Menagerie* (Royal Lyceum);
Stoopud Fucken Animals
(Traverse); *Mud* (Gate); *I
Caught Crabs in Walberswick*
(High Tide).
theatre whilst training
includes: *Caucasian Chalk
Circle*; *All's Well that Ends
Well* (RSC Complete Works
Festival).
film: *Pelican Blood*.
radio includes: *Dombey
and Son, Fortunes of War, All
Quiet on the Western Front,
Resurrection*.

MICHAEL BOYD
DIRECTOR
RSC: Michael has been Artistic
Director of the RSC since
2003. *The Histories Cycle,
The Broken Heart, Much Ado
About Nothing, The Spanish
Tragedy, Measure for Measure,
Troilus and Cressida, A
Midsummer Night's Dream,
Romeo and Juliet, Henry VI
Parts I, II* and *III, Richard III,
The Tempest, Hamlet,
Twelfth Night*.
this season: *As You Like It,
The Grain Store*.
trained: Malaya Bronnaya
Theatre, Moscow.
theatre includes: Michael Boyd
was the founding Artistic Director
of the Tron Theatre, Glasgow.
From 1982-84 he was Associate
Director of the Crucible Theatre,
Sheffield and from 1979-82
he was Director at the Belgrade
Theatre, Coventry. Other work
includes: *Miss Julie* (West
End); *Hedda Gabler* (Leicester
Haymarket); *Othello* (Lyric,
Hammersmith); *The Alchemist*
(Cambridge Theatre Co.).

ELYSE DODGSON
INTERNATIONAL
CONSULTANT
Elyse has been on the artistic
team of the Royal Court Theatre
since 1985, first as Director of
the Young People's Theatre and
from 1996 as Associate Director,
Head of International Department.
She has led play development
programmes for emerging

playwrights in all parts of the
world and produced dozens
of plays in International
Playwrights Seasons at the
Royal Court for more than a
decade. She is the founder
and director of the Royal
Court International Residency
which began in 1989 and
continues to bring international
playwrights to London every
summer. She began working
with Russian language
playwrights in 1999 and has
produced work by Vassily
Sigarev, The Presnyakov
Brothers and Natal'ia Vorozhbit
at the Royal Court.

SASHA DUGDALE
TRANSLATOR
RSC DEBUT SEASON: *The
Grain Store*.
Sasha is a poet and translator.
Her last collection, *The Estate*
(Carcanet/Oxford *Poets*),
was published in 2007. Her
translations of Elena Shvarts'
Birdsong on the Seabed was
a PBS Recommended Choice
and was shortlisted for the
2009 Rossica Prize. She has
translated over thirty Russian
plays and is a consultant in
Russian new writing for the
Royal Court. Her translations
of Vassily Sigarev and the
Presnyakov Brothers have been
produced at the Royal Court.
Her translation of Chekhov's
Cherry Orchard was broadcast
on BBC Radio 3.

NOMA DUMEZWENI

OLYANA

RSC: *Breakfast with Mugabe, Antony and Cleopatra, Much Ado about Nothing, Macbeth, trade.*
this season: Paulina in *The Winter's Tale,* Calphurnia in *Julius Caesar,* Olyana in *The Grain Store.*
theatre includes: *Six Characters in Search of an Author* (Chichester/West End); *The Master and Margarita, A Midsummer Night's Dream, The Coffee House, Nathan the Wise* (Chichester); *The Hour We Knew Nothing of Each Other, President of an Empty Room* (National Theatre); *A Raisin in the Sun* (Winner of the Olivier Award for Best Supporting Actor. Young Vic at the Lyric Hammersmith/tour); *Skellig, The Blacks* (Young Vic); *Ali Baba and the Forty Thieves, A Midsummer Night's Dream* (London Bubble).
television and film includes: *Doctor Who, Fallout, The Colour of Magic, Summerhill, EastEnders, Mysterious Creatures, The Last Enemy, New Tricks, Shameless, Holby City, Fallen Angel, After Thomas.*
radio includes: *No.1 Ladies*

Detective Agency, Pilgrim, A Time for Justice, The Farming of Bones.

OLIVER FENWICK
LIGHTING
DESIGNER
RSC DEBUT SEASON:
Julius Caesar, The Drunks, The Grain Store.
theatre includes: *Mary Stuart* (Hipp Theatre, Sweden); *Hedda Gabler* (Gate, Dublin); *Happy Now?* (National Theatre); *Private Lives, The Giant, Glass Eels, Comfort Me With Apples* (Hampstead); *The Lady from the Sea, She Stoops to Conquer* (Birmingham Rep); *The Elephant Man* (Sheffield Lyceum/tour); *Kean* (Apollo, West End); *Solid Gold Cadillac* (Garrick, West End); *The Secret Rapture* (Lyric, West End); *Far from the Madding Crowd* (ETT); *Jack and the Beanstalk* (Barbican Theatre); *Pure Gold* (Soho); *Henry V, Mirandolina, A Conversation* (Royal Exchange); *Restoration* (Headlong); *My Fair Lady* (Cameron Mackintosh/National Theatre tour); *The Caretaker* (Sheffield Crucible/Tricycle); *The Comedy of Errors, Bird Calls, Iphigenia* (Sheffield Crucible); *Endgame, Noises Off, All My Sons, Doctor Faustus* (Liverpool Playhouse).
opera includes: *Samson et Delilah, Lohengrin, The Trojan Trilogy, The Nose, The Gentle Giant* (Royal Opera House); *The Threepenny Opera* (The Opera Group); *L'Opera Seria* (Batignano Festival).

GEOFFREY FRESHWATER

LANDOWNER

RSC: *The Histories Cycle, The Taming of the Shrew, Julius Caesar, The Merchant of Venice, The Changeling, Coriolanus, Happy End, The Odyssey, Much Ado about Nothing, Richard III, Winter's Tale, King John, Jubilee, The Malcontent, The Roman Actor, Eastward Ho!, Thomas More, A New Way To Please You, Sejanus: His Fall.*
this season: Corin in *As You Like It,* Landowner in *The Grain Store.*
understudy: Feodosii/Samson.
theatre includes: *The Barber of Seville, The Tempest, The Way of the World, Dracula, Arsenic and Old Lace* (Chichester); *The Faerie Queen* (Aix-en-Provence); *The Invisible Man* (Stratford East); *The Churchill Play, The Mother, Merry Wives of Windsor, The Alchemist* (National Theatre); *Once in a Lifetime* (Piccadilly); *Piaf* (Wyndham's).
television includes: *The Professionals, Poirot, No Bananas, Trial and Retribution, Foyle's War, The Commander, Midsomer Murders, The Government Inspector.*

film includes: *A Bridge Too Far, The Grotesque, The Leading Man, Nocturnal, Sabotage.*
radio includes: *Patricia's Progress, Friends of Oscar, Top Story.*

television includes: *The Diary of Anne Frank, Oliver Twist, Skins.*
film: *Abraham's Point.*
radio includes: *Parthenogenesis, Regime Change.*

TRAMP

RSC: *Macbeth, Hamlet, Coriolanus, The Merry Wives of Windsor* (Old Vic/RSC), *Julius Caesar, Tantalus* (RSC/Denver Centre), *Family Reunion, Romeo and Juliet.*
this season: Leontes in *The Winter's Tale*, Julius Caesar in *Julius Caesar*, Tramp in *The Grain Store.*
understudy: Samoilenka/ Landowner.
trained: Rose Bruford.
theatre includes: *In Blood – The Bacchae, Small Craft Warnings, An Enemy of the People* (Arcola); *Don Quixote* (West Yorkshire Playhouse); *Angels in America* (Headlong/ Lyric Hammersmith); *The Lady of Leisure* (Liverpool Playhouse); *Missing Persons* (Trafalgar Studios/Assembly Rooms); *Tamburlaine the Great* (TMA Award for Best Performance in a Play. Bristol Old Vic/Barbican); *Messiah, King Lear, Waiting for Godot, The Seagull, Waste* (Old Vic); *The Bacchae, The Oedipus Plays* (and Greece), *Absolute Hell, The Cherry Orchard, The Duchess of Malfi, Coriolanus, Animal Farm, You Can't Take*

MASHA, AN ACTOR

RSC: *A Midsummer Night's Dream, Hamlet, Love's Labour's Lost, Antony and Cleopatra, Julius Caesar, The Tempest.*
this season: Celia in *As You Like It*, Courtesan in *The Comedy of Errors,* Masha, an Actor in *The Grain Store.*
trained: Guildhall School of Music and Drama.
theatre includes: *The Sea* (Theatre Royal Haymarket); *Vernon God Little* (Young Vic); *'Tis Pity She's A Whore* (Critics' Circle award for Most Promising Newcomer 2005. Time Out Live award for Best Newcomer 2005. Ian Charleson award 2005. Southwark Playhouse.); *Cymbeline, Twelfth Night* (Regent's Park); *Professor Bernhardi, Musik* (Arcola); *Much Ado about Nothing* (Globe); *The Lost Child* (Chichester); *Stealing Sweets and Punching People* (Latchmere).

LIONECHKA/ TODOS/GUARD

RSC DEBUT SEASON:
Young Shepherd in *The Winter's Tale*, Cinna the Conspirator/Young Cato in *Julius Caesar*, Lionechka/ Todos/Guard in *The Grain Store.*
understudy: Yukhim/ Gorobets/Guard.
trained: RADA (Winner of the Richard Burton Scholarship award).
theatre: *Romeo and Juliet* (Middle Temple Hall).

it with You, Lorenzaccio, Oresteia, The Spanish Tragedy (National Theatre).
television includes: Casualty, Trial and Retribution, Waking the Dead, Tiberius Gracchus, The Ten Commandments, Guardian, Jason and the Argonauts.

GAVRILO

RSC: Artistic Associate. Othello (as director), Everyman (RSC/BAM, New York).
this season: Gavrilo in The Grain Store, A Tender Thing.
work as a director includes: 4.48 Psychosis (LAMDA); The Birds (National Theatre); Destination (Volcano Theatre Co.); Wiseguy Scapino (Theatr Clwyd); Mr Puntila and his Man Matti (Almeida/Albery/Traverse); The Glory of Living (Royal Court); The Comedy of Errors, Pericles (Shakespeare's Globe).
work as a performer includes: Fragments (Young Vic/Bouffes du Nord/world tour); The Bee (Soho); The Maids (Brighton Festival); Yerma (Arcola); Celestina (Birmingham/

Edinburgh Festival); Whistling Psyche (Almeida); Richard III (Shakespeare's Globe); The Taming of the Shrew, Dona Rosita (Almeida); King Lear (Leicester Haymarket/Tokyo Globe); Macbeth, Electra (Leicester Haymarket); Far Away (Bouffes du Nord); The Rose Tattoo, The Devils (Theatr Clwyd); Live Like Pigs, The Recruiting Officer, Our Country's Good (Royal Court); Pericles, The Visit (Olivier Award for Best Actress. National Theatre). Theatre de Complicite includes: Foe, Help, I'm Alive!, The Winter's Tale.
film and television includes: Harry Potter and the Order of the Phoenix, All or Nothing, Wet and Dry, Orlando, Baby of Macon, Rome, Silent Witness.

ARSEI'S MOTHER

RSC: King John, Talk of the City (RSC/Young Vic), The Blue Angel (Olivier Award nomination for Best Actress in a Musical), Measure for Measure.
this season: Hermione in The Winter's Tale, Arsei's Mother The Grain Store.

understudy: Nurse/Lionechka's Mother.
theatre includes: Metamorphosis (Lyric Hammersmith); The Lucky Ones (Hampstead); Cuckoos (National Theatre Studio/Gate); Exquisite Sister (West Yorkshire Playhouse); As You Like It (TMA Best Actress Award), A Doll's House (English Touring Theatre); Trios (Riverside Studios); Not Fade Away (Bush); Trelawney of the Wells (tour/West End); Cabaret (Théâtre Mogadar, Paris); School for Scandal (Royal Exchange); Jean Seberg, She Stoops to Conquer, A Chorus of Disapproval (National Theatre); Don Giovanni (Greenwich); Evita (Prince Edward Theatre).
film includes: Golden Age, Vanity Fair, The Hole, The Luizhin Defence, Les Miserables.
radio includes: Number Ten, Soeur Sourire, Summerfolk, Henry VI, Talk of the City, Transit of Venus (Winner Sony Award for Best Dramatic Performance).

VASILII, AN ACTOR

RSC DEBUT SEASON: Le Beau in As You Like It, Vasilii,

an Actor in *The Grain Store*.
understudy: Yurko, an Actor/
Ivan Ivanovich, an Actor.
trained: Drama Centre, London.
theatre includes: *Wedding
Dance* (national tour);
*The Great Theatre of the
World* (Arcola); *Romeo and
Juliet* (Harlow Playhouse);
*Rosencrantz and Guildenstern
are Dead*, *Much Ado about
Nothing* (Library Theatre,
Manchester); *Blue/Orange*
(Cockpit); *Othello* (Upstairs at
the Gatehouse); *I'm an Asylum
Seeker – Get Me Into Here*
(Rosemary Branch); *Galileo*
(C Venue, Edinburgh).
television includes: *The Bill*,
Casualty, *10 Days to War*.

ARSEI PECHORITSA
RSC DEBUT SEASON:
Florizel in *The Winter's Tale*,
Romulus/Lucius in *Julius
Caesar*, Arsei Pechoritsa in
The Grain Store.
trained: Royal Scottish
Academy of Music and Drama.
theatre includes: *The
Brothers Size* (ATC/Young Vic);
The Cracks in My Skin (Royal
Exchange); *Big White Fog*
(Almeida); *Of Mice and Men*
(Oran Mor).
television: *Nearly Famous*.

TERRY KING
FIGHT DIRECTOR
RSC: Recent productions
include: *Othello*, *Hamlet*,
*A Midsummer Night's
Dream*, *The Histories
Cycle*, *Noughts & Crosses*,
Antony and Cleopatra,
Julius Caesar, *King John*,
Pericles, *The Indian Boy*,
Merry Wives: The Musical,
*A Midsummer Night's
Dream*, *Twelfth Night*, *As
You Like It*, *Gunpowder
Season*.
this season: *As You Like It*,
The Drunks, *The Grain Store*
theatre includes: *The Lord
of the Rings*, *On an Average
Day*, *Ragtime*, *Chitty Chitty
Bang Bang* (West End);
*Accidental Death of an
Anarchist*, *Caligula* (Donmar);
King Lear, *The Murderers*,
Fool for Love, *Duchess of
Malfi*, *Henry V*, *Edmund*,
Jerry Springer the Opera
(National Theatre); *Oleanna*,
Search and Destroy, *Sore
Throats* (Royal Court).
opera includes: *Othello*
(WNO); *Porgy and Bess*
(Glyndebourne); *West Side
Story* (York); *Carmen* (ENO).
television includes: *Fell
Tiger*, *A Kind of Innocence*,
A Fatal Inversion, *The Bill*,
EastEnders, *Measure for
Measure*, *Casualty*, *The
Widowing of Mrs. Holroyd*,
Death of a Salesman.

GAFIIKA/
LIONECHKA'S
MOTHER
RSC DEBUT SEASON:
Hisperia in *As You Like It*,
Luciana in *The Comedy of
Errors*, Gafiika/Lionechka's
Mother in *The Grain Store*.
understudy: Mokrina
Staritskaya/Kilina/Todos.
theatre includes: *Coram
Boy*, *A Matter of Life and Death*
(National Theatre); *Feathers
in the Snow* (National Theatre
Studio); *Cinderella* (Theatre
Royal, Stratford East); *Whistle
Down the Wind* (West End/
tour); *Sick!* (Almeida); *Ten
Suitcases* (Drill Hall); *Aida*
(Royal Albert Hall); *Carmen
Jones* (Old Vic); *The Vagina
Monologues* (Mercury,
Colchester); *The Count of
Monte Cristo* (West Yorkshire
Playhouse); *Saturday Night*
(White Bear); *Annie* (Edinburgh
Festival/National Youth Music
Theatre).
television includes: *Doctors*,
Casualty, *Holy Smoke*, *Night
and Day*, *Green Balloon Club*.

MORTKO

RSC: *The Histories Cycle, Twelfth Night, As You Like It, Pilate, Hamlet, Macbeth.*
this season: Camillo in *The Winter's Tale,* Cassius in *Julius Caesar,* Mortko in *The Grain Store.*
trained: Bristol Old Vic Theatre School.
theatre includes: *Six Characters in Search of an Author* (Headlong/West End); *Dark Earth* (Traverse); *All My Sons* (York Theatre Royal); *War Music* (Sound and Fury); *Troilus and Cressida, As You Like It, The Winter's Tale, Twelfth Night, Coriolanus, Measure for Measure, A Midsummer Night's Dream, King Lear* (Shakespeare at the Tobacco Factory).
television includes: *Law and Order UK, Doc Martin, Trial and Retribution, Casualty, London's Burning.*
radio includes: *Heart of Darkness, Night and Day, Madeleine, Soldier Soldier, Evelina, The Iliad, Poetry Please.*

SAMSON

RSC: *The Histories Cycle, Twelfth Night, The Comedy of Errors, Macbeth, Hamlet, The Pilate Workshop.*
this season: Jaques in *As You Like It,* Samson in *The Grain Store, A Tender Thing.*
trained: RSAMD.
theatre includes: *King Lear* (Liverpool Everyman/Young Vic); *The Breathing House, Art, Much Ado about Nothing* (Lyceum, Edinburgh); *San Diego, Dumbstruck, Cinzano, Endgame* (Tron); *A Wee Bit of How Do You Do, Sounds of Progress, The Trick is to Keep Breathing* (Tron/Toronto/Royal Court); *The Real World* (Tron/New York); *Laurel and Hardy* (Edinburgh/New Zealand); *The Life of Stuff* (Donmar).
television includes: *No Holds Bard, EastEnders, The High Life, Hamish Macbeth, Red Dwarf.*
radio includes: *McLevy, Forbes Masson Half Hour, The Trick is to Keep Breathing, Conan Doyle - A Life in Letters.*
writing includes: *Stiff!, Mince?* (also directed. Nominated for Best Musical, TMA Awards 2001), *Pants* (also directed).
Forbes is an Associate Artist of The National Theatre of Scotland.

ANNA MORRISSEY
MOVEMENT DIRECTOR

RSC: *The Cordelia Dream, The Tragedy of Thomas Hobbes, I'll be the Devil* (RSC/Tricycle), *Timon of Athens* (RSC/Cardboard Citizens).
theatre and opera includes: *Hansel and Gretel* (Opera North); *Hanover Square* (Finborough); *101 Dalmatians* (Theatre Royal, Northampton); *The Barber of Seville, Manon Lescaut* (Opera Holland Park); *Dr Faustus* (Resolution! The Place); *The Tempest, A Warwickshire Testimony, As You Like It, Macbeth* (Bridge House); *The Taming of the Shrew* (Creation Theatre Co.); *Richard III* (Cambridge Arts); *Hamlet* (Cliffords Tower, York); *The Arab-Israeli Cookbook* (Tricycle); *Human Rites* (Southwark Playhouse); *Julius Caesar* (Menier Chocolate Factory); *Tamburlaine the Great* (Rose).
Anna has worked as a practitioner within the RSC Movement Department and taught at E15, Queen Mary and Westfield and Shakespeare's Globe Education.

DHARMESH PATEL

ONIS'KO

RSC DEBUT SEASON: Lord Amiens in *As You Like It*, Angelo in *The Comedy of Errors*, Onis'ko in *The Grain Store*.
understudy: Arsei Pechoritsa/Lionechka.
trained: Hope Street Physical Theatre School.
theatre includes: *Happy and Married?*, *Silent Cry* (Freedom Studios); *Satyagraha* (Improbable); *Beauty and the Beast*, *Accidental Death of an Anarchist* (Told by an Idiot); *Too Close to Home* (RASA); *Slowtime* (National Theatre); *The Happy Prince*, *Bollywood Jane* (Haymarket, Leicester); *No Fear*, *The Government Inspector*, *Beauty and the Beast* (Unity Theatre).
television includes: *Casualty*, *Doctors*, *Ray's Daze*.
radio includes: *Jefferson 37*, *Silver Street*, *Whimmy Road*.

TOM PIPER
DESIGNER

RSC designs include: *The Histories Cycle*, *Macbeth*, *The Broken Heart*, *Spring Awakening*, *A Patriot for Me*, *Much Ado about Nothing*, *The Spanish Tragedy*, *Bartholomew Fair*, *Measure for Measure*, *Troilus and Cressida*, *A Month in the Country*, *A Midsummer Night's Dream*, *Romeo and Juliet*, *Henry VI*, *Richard III*, *The Tempest*, *King Lear*, *Twelfth Night*, *Hamlet*.
this season: *As You Like It*, *The Grain Store*, *The Drunks*.
theatre designs include: *The Birthday Party*, *Blinded by the Sun*, *Oh! What a Lovely War* (National Theatre); *Miss Julie* (Haymarket); *Frame 312*, *A Lie of the Mind*, *Three Days of Rain*, *Helpless* (Donmar); *Pants*, *Mince?*, *Duchess of Malfi*, *Twelfth Night*, *Happy Days* (Dundee Rep); *Denial*, *Les Liaisons Dangereuses*, *Ghosts* (Bristol Old Vic); *The Danny Crowe Show* (Bush); *The Frogs*, *The Cherry Orchard* (Nottingham Playhouse); *Stiff!*, *The Master Builder* (Lyceum, Edinburgh); *The Crucible*, *Six Characters in Search of an Author* (Abbey, Dublin); *Backpay*, *Cockroach, Who?* (Royal Court); *Zorro* (Garrick); *Spyski!* (Lyric Hammersmith); *Dealer's Choice* (Menier Chocolate Factory/Trafalgar); *Fall* (Traverse).

NICK POWELL
SOUND DESIGNER

RSC: *The Big Lie* (Latitude Festival), *God in Ruins* (RSC/Soho).
this season: *The Drunks*, *The Grain Store*.
theatre includes: As composer and sound designer: *Panic* (Improbable); *The Vertical Hour*, *Relocated* (Royal Court); *Bonheur* (Composer. Comedie Francais, Paris). Music and songs for: *Urtain*, *Marat/Sade* (Spanish National Theatre/Animalario); *Realism* (Edinburgh International Festival); *The Wonderful World of Dissocia* (Winner of Best Production for TMA and Scottish Theatre awards); *Pyrenees* (TMA Best New Play), *Mercury Fur*, *The Drowned World*, *Tiny Dynamite* (co-produced with Frantic Assembly), *Splendour* (Paines Plough). Co-creator and composer: *The Wolves in the Walls* (National Theatre of Scotland/Improbable). As Musical Director of Glasgow's Suspect Culture Nick developed and scored twelve shows including *Timeless*, *Mainstream*, *Casanova*, *Lament*, *One, Two…*, *800m* and *Futurology: A Global Review* as well as numerous workshops and performances throughout the world.
film and television includes: *Beneath the Veil* (BAFTA winner), *Luther*, *Death in Gaza* (BAFTA winner).
music includes: He is one half of Oskar, who have just released *LP:2*, the follow-up to their debut album *Air Conditioning*.

PATRICK ROMER

ARTIUKH THE BURIER/OLD WOMAN DANCING

RSC: *Much Ado about Nothing, Romeo and Juliet, Julius Caesar, The Two Gentlemen of Verona, The Merry Wives of Windsor, Coriolanus.*
this season: Time/Mariner/Servant in *The Winter's Tale,* Murullus/Publius/Cinna the Poet/Clitus in *Julius Caesar,* Artiukh the Burier/Old Woman Dancing in *The Grain Store.*
understudy: Tramp/Old Woman with an Empty Bucket.
trained: Rose Bruford.
theatre includes: *The Masque of the Red Death* (Punchdrunk); *Bulletproof Soul* (Birmingham Rep); *The Comedy of Errors* (Bristol Old Vic); *Mirita* (Finborough); *La Cava* (Piccadilly); *An Enemy of the People, Peter Pan* (National Theatre); *The Tailor-Made Man* (Cockpit); *Of Mice and Men* (Coventry Belgrade); *The Cid, Twelfth Night* (Cheek by Jowl/tour). Patrick has also been involved in over 60 productions for the Northcott Theatre, Exeter and over 12 productions for the

Lyceum Theatre, Crewe.
television includes: *Primeval, Robinson Crusoe, The Four Seasons, Casualty, The Bill.*
film: *The World is Not Enough.*
radio includes: *All Passion Spent,* regular reader on *Poetry Please,* reader for RNIB's talking books.

DAVID RUBIN

YUKHIM

RSC: *Antony and Cleopatra, Julius Caesar, The Tempest.*
this season: Sicilian Lord in *The Winter's Tale,* Trebonius/Lucilius in *Julius Caesar,* Yukhim in *The Grain Store.*
understudy: Mortko.
theatre includes: *Fightface* (Lyric Hammersmith); *As the Mother of a Brown Boy, Hamlet, The Attraction, Paula's Story* (Chickenshed); *The Overcoat, Taylor's Dummies* (Gecko); *The Red Balloon, Threepenny Opera, A Midsummer Night's Dream, As You Like It, The Tempest,* two productions of *Twelfth Night* (National Theatre); *Five Guys Named Moe* (Lyric); *In the Midnight Hour* (Young Vic); *Godspell* (Barbican); *Macbeth* (Chester Gateway); *Cyrano de Bergerac* (Theatre Royal, Northampton); *Company,*

Duck Variations (New Wolsey, Ipswich); *The Legend of King Arthur* (Red Shift); *100* (The Imaginary Body); *Sharrow Stories* (Sheffield Crucible); *The Wizard of Oz* (Oldham Coliseum); *Peter Pan* (Nuffield, Southampton); *Stomp* (Royal Festival Hall).
television includes: *The Passion, Holby City, Walking With Cavemen, EastEnders, Dalziel and Pascoe, Sitting Pretty, Mysteries of July, Running Time, Number 73, Watch, Good Health, Playdays.*
film includes: *Brooms, Crossover, After a Time.*
David was a founder member of The Company at Chickenshed Theatre and is a Freelance Associate Practitioner for the RSC.

OLIVER RYAN

GOROBETS

RSC DEBUT SEASON:
Servant in *The Winter's Tale,* Casca/Pindarus in *Julius Caesar,* Gorobets in *The Grain Store.*
understudy: Gavrilo.
theatre includes: *Memory* (Theatr Clwyd/The Pleasance, New York); *Macbeth, Arcadia, One Flew Over the Cuckoo's Nest, The Crucible, Rosencrantz*

and Guildenstern are Dead, The Rabbit, King Lear, Of Mice and Men, Afore Night Come, Equus (Theatr Clwyd); Nostalgia (Plymouth Drum); Past Away (Sgript Cymru); Richard II, Coriolanus (Almeida/New York/Tokyo); Unprotected Sex, Everything Must Go (Sherman Theatre); Hamlet (Birmingham Rep).

television includes: Casualty, Midsomer Murders, Caerdydd, Doctors, A Harlot's Progress, High Hopes, The Bill, Life and Debt, Nuts and Bolts, The Bench, A Mind to Kill, Holby City, Jack of Hearts.
film: Killing Me Softly.

SIMONE SAUNDERS

MOKRINA'S SISTER/ NURSE

RSC DEBUT SEASON: Dorcas/Lady in The Winter's Tale, Calphurnia's Servant in Julius Caesar, Mokrina's Sister/Nurse in The Grain Store.
understudy: Onis'ko/Arsei's Mother.
trained: East 15.
theatre includes: Claudia Jones (Talawa Theatre); The Tempest (Northern Broadsides); Double Take (Nottingham Playhouse/Red

Earth); The Red Ladies (Clod Ensemble/National Theatre); Goodnight Desdemona, Good Morning Juliet (Toucan Theatre Co.).

PETER SHOREY

OLD WOMAN WITH AN EMPTY BUCKET

RSC: The Merchant of Venice, The Taming of the Shrew, The Tragedy of Thomas Hobbes.
this season: Adam in As You Like It, Old Woman with an Empty Bucket in The Grain Store.
understudy: Old Woman Dancing.
theatre includes: Measure for Measure, Twelfth Night, The Golden Ass, Richard II, Edward II (Shakespeare's Globe/USA tour). Seasons at Theatre by the Lake Keswick, Watford Palace, New Vic Stoke, Theatre Royal Northampton, Dukes Lancaster, Theatre Royal York, Salisbury Playhouse, Nottingham Playhouse, Oldham Coliseum, Mercury Theatre Colchester, Birmingham Rep, Northcott Exeter, Belgrade Coventry, Gateway Chester, Warehouse Theatre Croydon, BAC, Avon Touring, Torch Milford Haven and The Drill Hall, London.

television includes: Compromised Immunity, Black and White and Read All Over, Patagonia, Mr Codger, Minder, The Bill.
writing includes: Jack and the Beanstalk, Babes in the Wood, Dick Whittington (Mercury, Colchester); Cinderella (Theatre Royal, Northampton).

VIK SIVALINGAM ASSISTANT DIRECTOR

RSC: Romeo and Juliet.
this season: The Comedy of Errors, The Grain Store.
trained: Birkbeck, University of London.
theatre includes: As Director: Or Nearest Offer (Almeida); Daisy Pulls It Off (Cockpit); Three Sisters (Actors Company); Memories of Midnights Gone (Bull Theatre); Elephant Man (Associate Director. Sheffield Theatres tour); Jack and the Beanstalk (Stafford Gatehouse); When the Lights Went Out (Tara Arts); Broom – Just Say No, Parklife: Achieving Liberty, Head Over Heels (Pulse Festival, Ipswich); Travels to Myself (Teatro Technis); Please Find Attached (King's Head); The Waiting Line (Birmingham ArtsFest); The Hard Way (Soho Studio); Human Rights (Sir John Mills, Ipswich); Blue/Orange (New Wolsey Studio); Girlfriends (Co-director. BAC); Day Trippers (New Wolsey Theatre/ Theatr Clwyd); Swingin' In Mid-Dream! (Albany, London). As Assistant Director: Free Outgoing (Royal Court); The Last Days of Judas Iscariot

(Almeida); *Rough Crossings* (Headlong); *The Soldier's Fortune* (Young Vic); *The Price, Private Lives, The Tempest, Sugar* (New Wolsey).

KATY STEPHENS

SAMOILENKA
RSC: *The Histories Cycle.*
this season: Rosalind in *As You Like It,* Samoilenka in *The Grain Store.*
understudy: Olyana/Rudenko, the Educator.
trained: National Youth Theatre, Welsh College of Music and Drama.
theatre includes: *Tamburlaine* (Bristol Old Vic/Barbican); *The Seagull, Ion, Macbeth, The White Devil, Oh! What a Lovely War, The Three Sisters, The Europeans, Caucasian Chalk Circle, Blood Wedding, The Recruiting Officer* (Mercury, Colchester); *Twelfth Night, Sleeping Beauty, Our Day Out, Silas Marner* (Belgrade, Coventry); *David Copperfield, I Don't Want to Set the World on Fire* (New Victoria, Newcastle); *A Midsummer Night's Dream* (Orchard Theatre Co.).
television includes: *The Bill, London's Burning, Ellington, Fun Song Factory, Wow.*
film: *Relative Values.*

SAM TROUGHTON

IVAN IVANOVICH, AN ACTOR
RSC: *A Midsummer Night's Dream* (RSC/City of London Sinfonia), *Richard III* (Ian Charleson award nomination), *Henry VI Parts I, II* and *III* (Ian Charleson award nomination), *The Taming of the Shrew.*
this season: Dion/Paulina's Steward in *The Winter's Tale,* Marcus Brutus in *Julius Caesar,* Ivan Ivanovich, an Actor in *The Grain Store.*
understudy: Yurko, an Actor.
theatre includes: *An Oak Tree* (Birmingham Rep); *As You Like It* (Sheffield Crucible); *Nathan the Wise* (Hampstead); *Buried Child, The Coast of Utopia: Voyage, Shipwreck, Salvage, Tartuffe* (Ian Charleson award nomination) (National Theatre); *School for Scandal* (Derby Playhouse); *A Midsummer Night's Dream* (Cannizaro Park); *The Other Shore* (Attic Theatre Co.); *Confidence* (The Water Melon); *Hamlet* (Orange Tree); *The Bald Prima Donna* (Best Actor NSDF. Edinburgh NSTC).
television includes: *Robin Hood, Hex II, Messiah III,*

Gunpowder, Treason and Plot, Judge John Deed, Ultimate Force, Foyle's War.
film includes: *Spirit Trap, Alien vs. Predator, Vera Drake, Sylvia.*

JAMES TUCKER

RUDENKO, THE EDUCATOR
RSC: *The Histories Cycle, Eastward Ho!, The Malcontent, Edward III, The Island Princess, Henry VI Parts I, II* and *III, Richard III, The Lion, the Witch and the Wardrobe, The Two Gentlemen of Verona, Bartholomew Fair, Measure for Measure, Seeds Under Stones, A Woman of No Importance.*
this season: Silvius in *As You Like It,* Antipholus of Ephesus in *The Comedy of Errors,* Rudenko, the Educator in *The Grain Store.*
theatre includes: *Ivanov* (Donmar Warehouse at Wyndham's); *The Winter's Tale, Twelfth Night, Henry V* (Propeller at the Watermill Theatre. UK and world tours); *Hamlet* (UK tour); *A Midsummer Night's Dream* (Sheffield Crucible); *Hinge of the World* (Yvonne Arnaud);

The Cherry Orchard (English
Touring Theatre); The Tempest
(Nottingham Playhouse/
world tour); Hamlet (Glasgow
Citizens); Twelfth Night
(Nottingham Playhouse);
Shadowlands (national tour); A
Month in the Country (Albery).
television includes: Agatha
Christie: A Life in Pictures,
Silent Witness.

NATAL'IA VOROZHBIT
WRITER

Natal'ia Vorozhbit was born in
Kiev, Ukraine and studied at the
Moscow Literary Institute. Two
of her plays, Demons and Galka
Motalko, have been staged in
Moscow, St. Petersburg, the
National Theatre of Latvia and
other theatres of Russia and
Ukraine. Galka Motalko has
been adapted for screen and
is currently being filmed in
Moscow. The Khomenko Family
Chronicles was commissioned
jointly by the Royal Court and
the BBC World Service. It was
first performed as a rehearsed
reading as part of Small Talk:
Big Picture at the Royal Court
in 2006. It was then staged
as part of the Royal Court's
International Season in Winter
2007 in a double bill with The
Good Family by Joakim Pirinen.

LARRINGTON **WALKER**

FEODOSII/GUARD
RSC: The Merchant of
Venice, The Taming of the
Shrew, The Tragedy of
Thomas Hobbes.
this season: Old Shepherd
in The Winter's Tale,
Soothsayer/Octavius'
Servant/Strato in Julius
Caesar, Feodosii/Guard in
The Grain Store.
understudy: Guard/Artiukh
the Burier.
theatre includes: Jenufa
(Arcola); Daddy Cool
(Shaftesbury/Berlin); Ska
Ba Day (Greenwich/Talawa);
Pinocchio, Old Time Story
(Theatre Royal, Stratford East);
Playboy of the West Indies
(Tricycle/Nottingham); Stuff
Happens, The Beggar's Opera,
Guys and Dolls (National
Theatre); Blues for Mr. Charlie
(Wolsey/Tricycle); Driving Miss
Daisy (Oldham Coliseum);
Wrong Time Right Place (Soho
Theatre Co.); Whistle Down
the Wind (tour); The Free State
(Birmingham Rep/tour); The
Merchant of Venice (West
Yorkshire Playhouse); Lost in
the Stars (New Sussex Opera,
Brighton); Week In Week Out
(Foco Novo/Soho Poly).

television includes: The Bill,
Beck, Peak Practice, Inspector
Morse, Playdays, Tecx, You and
Me, Thin Air.
film includes: Human Traffic,
Lamb, Burning Illusion, Yanks.
radio includes: Equiano,
Whose is the Kingdom?,
Rudy's Rare Records.

KIRSTY **WOODWARD**

KILINA
RSC DEBUT SEASON:
Mopsa/Lady in The Winter's
Tale, Priestess in Julius
Caesar, Kilina in The Grain
Store.
understudy: Masha, an
Actor.
trained: National Youth Theatre
and Kneehigh Theatre.
theatre includes: Beauty and
the Beast (Told by an Idiot/
Warwick Arts Centre). With
Kneehigh Theatre: Cymbeline
(RSC Complete Works
Festival/Lyric Hammersmith/
national tour/Brazil/Columbia),
Rapunzel (BAC/Queen
Elizabeth Hall), A Matter of Life
and Death (National Theatre),
Blast (national tour).

JOHN WOOLF
COMPOSER/MUSIC DIRECTOR

RSC: John is RSC Head of Music. He joined the wind band in 1977, and was appointed Music Director for Stratford in 1987. Since then he has been MD on most of Shakespeare's plays and other productions including: *Fair Maid of the West* (1987 Royal opening of the Swan), *The Wizard of Oz, The Beggar's Opera, Faust, The Lion, the Witch and the Wardrobe, The Secret Garden, Beauty and the Beast.*

this season: *As You Like It, The Grain Store.*

trained: Read music at St John's, Cambridge and Royal Academy of Music, studying oboe with Janet Craxton. Winner of 1970 York Bowen Prize.

as composer/arranger work includes: *The Quest, Moliere, Twin Rivals, Measure for Measure, Seeds Under Stones, Troilus and Cressida, A Midsummer Night's Dream, Timon of Athens, Miss Julie* (West End); *The Tempest, Twelfth Night, Hamlet, The Histories Cycle.*

film: MD for Trevor Nunn's *Twelfth Night.*

SAMANTHA YOUNG

MOKRINA STARITSKAYA

RSC: *I'll be the Devil.*

this season: Perdita in *The Winter's Tale*, Soothsayer's Acolyte in *Julius Caesar,* Mokrina Staritskaya in *The Grain Store.*

trained: RSAMD.

theatre includes: *Videotape* (Oran Mor); *Fall* (Traverse, Edinburgh); *Hamlet* (Glasgow Citizens); *Europe* (Dundee Rep/Barbican); *Gobbo, Miss Julie, The Crucible* (National Theatre of Scotland); *A Taste of Honey* (Tag); *The Graduate, The Visit, A Lie of the Mind, Macbeth* (Dundee Rep); *Snow White* (Glasgow Citizens).

television includes: *Casualty, River City.*

short film: *Mono.*

radio includes: *Freefalling, Look Back in Anger, Almost Blue.*

Production Acknowledgments

Scenery, set painting, properties, costumes, armoury, wigs and make-up by RSC Workshops, Stratford-upon-Avon. Joe Hull of High Performance Rigging with Steve Robinson. Richard Boles, Wyre Area Forester, Forestry Commission. Additional costumes made by Jamie Attle and Glenda Sharpe. Production photographer Ellie Kurttz. Access performances provided by Ellie Packer, Julia Grundy and Ridanne Sheridan. With thanks to Dr. Ljudmila Pekarska and Volodymyr Muzyczka from the Association of Ukrainians in Great Britain; Vitaly Lysenko; Vlodko Hnatiw and Iryna Hnatiw; Svitlana; Leon Fairbank, Aaron Foster and Artur Cichowski from Digby Trout Restaurants for food preparation; Natalie Heysa and Rozanna Madylus for help with Ukrainian pronunciation; and to Sainsbury's for generously providing the food used in each performance.

SUPPORT THE RSC

As a registered charity the Royal Shakespeare Company relies on public support and generosity.

There are many ways you can help the RSC including joining Shakespeare's Circle, RSC Patrons, through Corporate support or by leaving a bequest.

RSC Patrons and Shakespeare's Circle

By supporting the RSC through Shakespeare's Circle and RSC Patrons you can help us to create outstanding theatre and give as many people as possible a richer and fuller understanding of Shakespeare and theatre practice. In return you receive benefits including priority booking and invitations to exclusive supporters' events. Shakespeare's Circle Membership starts at £8.50 per month.

Help Secure our Future

Legacy gifts ensure that the RSC can develop and flourish in the years to come, bringing the pleasure of theatre to future generations that you yourself have enjoyed.

Corporate Partnerships

The RSC has a national and internationally recognised brand, whilst retaining its unique positioning as a Warwickshire-based organisation. It tours more than any other UK-based arts organisation and has annual residencies in London and Newcastle upon Tyne. As such it is uniquely placed to offer corporate partnership benefits across the globe.

The Company's experienced Corporate Development team can create bespoke packages around their extensive range of classical and new work productions, education programmes and online activity. These are designed to fulfil business objectives such as building client relationships, encouraging staff retention and accessing specific segments of the RSC's audience. A prestigious programme of corporate hospitality and membership packages are also available.

For more information, please telephone **01789 403470**.

For detailed information about opportunities to support the work of the RSC visit **www.rsc.org.uk/support**

TRANSFORMING OUR
THEATRES

In 1932, following the 1926 fire which destroyed much of the original Shakespeare Memorial Theatre, a new proscenium arch space opened in Stratford-upon-Avon, designed by Elizabeth Scott. Now known as the Royal Shakespeare Theatre the building boasted a spacious, fan-shaped auditorium housed inside Scott's art-deco inspired designs.

And now the RST is undergoing another transformation from a proscenium stage to a one-room space allowing the epic and intimate to play side by side.

At the heart of the project will be a new auditorium. Seating around 1,000 people, the stage thrusts into the audience with theatregoers seated on three sides, bringing the actor and audience closer together for a more intimate theatre experience.

The new space will transform the existing theatre, retaining the key Art Deco elements of the building. A new Theatre Tower with viewing platform, theatre square for outdoor performances, a linking foyer to join the Royal Shakespeare and Swan Theatres together for the first time, and new public spaces are central to the new building.

7,000 people have already supported the transformation from over 40 countries worldwide. To find out more and to play your part visit **www.rsc.org.uk/appeal**

GET MORE INVOLVED

RSC Membership

Become an RSC Member and enjoy a wide range of benefits.

Full Member £36 (per year).
As an RSC Full Member you receive up to four weeks' priority booking with a dedicated hotline into the RSC Box Office, Director's selection of four exclusive production photographs per year, regular Members' newsletters, access to Members' only web pages, special ticket offers – save £20 on two top price tickets in Stratford (conditions apply) and 10% discount in RSC Shops, Mail Order, RSC Short Breaks and at The Courtyard Theatre Café Bar.

Associate Member £15 (per year).
As an RSC Associate Member you receive priority booking of up to two weeks with a dedicated hotline into the RSC Box Office, regular Members' newsletters and 10% discount in The Courtyard Theatre Café Bar and with RSC Short Breaks.

Gift Membership.
All membership levels can be bought as a gift.

Overseas Membership.
This is available for those living outside the UK.

To find out more or to join, please contact the Membership Office on **01789 403440** (Monday-Friday 9am-5pm) or visit **www.rsc.org.uk/membership**

GET MORE INVOLVED

RSC Friends

As a network of the RSC's most active supporters, RSC Friends are important advocates for the Company, encouraging people to enjoy a closer relationship with the RSC and its work on and off stage.

Joining the Friends costs £20 a year and is open to RSC Full and Associate Members. Benefits include a lively programme of events plus a quarterly Friends' Newsletter and further opportunities to become more closely involved with the RSC.

For more information or to join, please contact the Membership Office on **01789 403440** or join online at **www.rsc.org.uk/membership**

RSC Online

www.rsc.org.uk

Visit the RSC website to Select Your Own Seat and book tickets online, keep up to date with the latest news, sign up for regular email updates or simply learn more about Shakespeare in our Exploring Shakespeare section.

THE ROYAL SHAKESPEARE COMPANY

Patron
Her Majesty the Queen

President
His Royal Highness The Prince of Wales

Deputy President
Sir Geoffrey Cass

Artistic Director
Michael Boyd

Executive Director
Vikki Heywood

Board
Sir Christopher Bland (*Chairman*)
Professor Jonathan Bate FBA FRSL CBE
Michael Boyd (*Artistic Director*)
David Burbidge OBE
Jane Drabble OBE
Noma Dumezweni
Mark Foster
Gilla Harris
Vikki Heywood (*Executive Director*)
John Hornby
Laurence Isaacson CBE
Jonathan Kestenbaum
Paul Morrell
Tim Pigott-Smith
Neil Rami
Lady Sainsbury of Turville (*Deputy Chairman*)

The RSC was established in 1961. It is incorporated under Royal Charter and is a registered charity, number 212481.

THE GRAIN STORE

Natal'ia Vorozhbit

Translated by Sasha Dugdale

And if you do come and visit, then we'll serve you melon, the likes of which I don't suppose you'll ever have tasted. And the honey, well, I swear you won't find better in any village. When I bring the honeycomb into the house, the scent fills the room; you can't possibly imagine it – pure as a teardrop, or an expensive crystal, like they have in earrings. And the pies my old lady serves up! Well, you've no idea. Nectar, they are, nectar, pure and perfect! The butter drips all over your lips when you bite into them. These ladies – what they can't do is nobody's business. Now, gentlemen, have you ever drunk pear and rosehip beer, or prune and raisin punch? Or have you ever been lucky enough to try Lenten porridge with milk? Goodness me, there's nothing like it in the world! You start eating, and that's it, you can't stop. The indescribable sweetness! Come and visit, and don't take your time; and we'll feed you so you can't help but stop strangers on the street to tell them about it...

From *Evenings on a Farm Near Dikanka* by Nikolai Gogol

4

Characters

MOKRINA STARITSKAYA
ARSEI PECHORITSA
MORTKO, *the regional government representative*
FEODOSII, *Mokrina's father*
OLIANA, *Mokrina's mother*
ODARKA, *Arsei's mother*
SAMSON ⎫
GOROBETS ⎰ *two friends*
KILINA
RUDENKO, *the local educator*
ARTYUKH, *the gravedigger*
SAMOILENKO, *the flesheater*
OLD WOMAN *with an empty bucket*
NURSE
LYONECHKA, *a fourteen-year-old boy*
OLD MAN *and* WOMAN
TRAMP

MOKRINA'S RELATIVES AND FELLOW VILLAGERS
KHRASINA, SEKLETA, YAKIM, BRONIA, FYODORA,
MINA, YAVDOKHA, TODOS, YUGINA, GORPINA,
YAVDOKHA, TEKLIA, SAFON, ONIS'KO, PROKOP,
STASYA, KHRANKA, TOFILIA, YANIK, FANAS, GAFIIKA

AGITATORS
IVAN IVANYCH, YURKO, MASHA, VASILII

POLITICAL ACTIVISTS
GAVRILO, YUKHIM

Plus various other VILLAGERS, HOSPITAL PATIENTS

*This text went to press before the end of rehearsals and so may
differ slightly from the play as performed.*

ACT ONE

16 August 1929

Peasant Feodosii's yard.

A long wooden table in the cherry orchard, with benches on either side.

The table groans under the weight of the feast: weeping sliced melons, piping-hot potatoes, freshly dug vegetables, fried meat.

There is no one at the table and only the pretty flies are hanging over the food. They buzz and make lazy landings on it.

Everyone is sitting with their backs to the table, watching the AGITATORS' *performance.*

They are performing a play, titled: FOR THE FEAR OF GOD!

On the imaginary stage there is a poster with a large icon pictured on it.

IVAN IVANYCH.
>Will wonders never cease!
>Mary from her icon speaks!
>From all around they dodge and weave,
>To look the icon in the teeth.

The AGITATORS *enter, playing peasants. They take it in turns to pray before the speaking icon.*

PEASANT. O Lord, grant me health, and grant my wife and children health, too!

ICON.
>Pay me lots and lots and lots,
>In no time at all you'll be strong like an ox!

PEASANT GIRL. My beloved no longer loves me. Lord, what should I do?

ICON. A few coins should do the trick.

PEASANT.
>And my cow, help me, Mary, please –
>She has a fungus on her knees.

ICON. If that's true, a note or two...

AGITATOR.
>But along comes an atheist.
>He pulls back the icon.
>And behind it, the priest and his wife are counting
>money –

PRIEST'S WIFE.
>This'll go on lace and trim,
>This on spoons and such.

AGITATOR.
>The priest gives his wife a knocking-about,
>And there she is: all stretched out –
>That's the last he'll hear from her!
>He hides the money under his skirts,
>To keep him a while in drink and girls.

AGITATOR.
>Good people, hear my word:
>There is no Lord!
>Take heed,
>Comrades, friends,
>And for all your needs,
>Ask the Soviet!

The YOUNGER PEOPLE *giggle and clap the* ACTORS.
The OLD WOMEN *cross themselves quietly.*

FEODOSII *looks sternly at his daughter* MOKRINA, *who is laughing together with everyone else.*

GOROBETS. They're good, those actors! Could be talking about our priest's wife.

SAMSON. Bless her memory...

SAMSON *crosses himself three times.* MASHA, *an agitator, who has been giving him little glances, notices this.*

MASHA. Hey, you, big fellow, do you cross yourself when you're in bed with a woman, too?

SAMSON. Better believe it! Three times before and three after. And I make the sign of the cross on her. Like putting pepper on my soup, it's that natural.

MASHA. Well, just so you know, I like pepper and all.

She shoots long looks at SAMSON *with her beautiful eyes.*

GOROBETS. Look at that, Samson, you've made an impression on their actress. Aren't you a lucky boy…

SAMSON. Ah, she can go to the Devil for all I care, God forgive me. As long as I'm well fed, it's all the same to me, an actress or an old hunchback. No, you tell me this, Gorobets, is it true that the new powers-that-be are going to knock down all the churches and build red towers in their place?

GOROBETS. Heaven forbid!

GOROBETS *spits three times over each shoulder.*

Handsome ARSEI, *who is standing next to* MOKRINA, *begins flirting with her.*

ARSEI. Mokrina, when you grow up we'll run away with the agit-brigades. See the whole of Soviet Ukraine!

MOKRINA. Tsk! I'm not going anywhere with you.

ARSEI. But I thought you loved me?

MOKRINA. Like a dog loves a whip.

ARSEI. Well then?

MOKRINA. You haven't asked them, Arsei.

ARSEI. I spoke to the man in charge. He promised to take me.

MOKRINA. I'm scared.

ARSEI. Of me? Kilina isn't scared.

MOKRINA. Ha! Well, you take your Kilina with you, then!

MOKRINA *gets up and runs away, angry and hurt*.

ARSEI. Oh, come on! I was joking! I don't want any old Kilina!

MOKRINA *runs away from* ARSEI *and runs onto the improvised stage by mistake*. IVAN IVANYCH *seizes her around the waist*.

IVAN IVANYCH. And now this pretty little lassie is going to tell us everything she knows about God and about collective farms.

MOKRINA *squeals and tries to escape*.

MOKRINA. Oh Lord, let me go…

IVAN IVANYCH. 'Lord', is it? No, my name is Ivan Ivanych. So, child, you tell me, does God exist?

MOKRINA (*still shy, but slyly peeping at him with black eyes*). Someone do away with Him, did they?

The CROWD *laughs*.

IVAN IVANYCH (*laughing*). Course they did. Soviet power.

MOKRINA. Did they ask God first?

IVAN IVANYCH. Sent Him a letter. But the letter came back unopened. So He can't exist, seeing as He never read the letter.

MOKRINA. Maybe He just didn't want to read it, when He saw it was from you.

The CROWD *and the* AGITATORS *burst into laughter*.

IVAN IVANYCH. Or maybe He couldn't read?

MOKRINA. You'd be better off praying to Him and not writing.

IVAN IVANYCH (*kindly*). Such a pretty, clever little lassie, and she says such silly things. Never mind. I'll be back in a year or two. What will you say then?

MOKRINA. I'll wish you your good health, Ivan Ivanych.

IVAN IVANYCH. And I wish you yours, my beauty. What can we have from you, then? Can you sing?

OLD WOMAN. Sing for us, Mokrina.

EVERYONE. Sing for us.

MOKRINA, *pensive, begins singing a sad song which doesn't seem to fit the cheerful mood, the laughter and the feast on the table.*

MOKRINA (*singing*).
Woe, woe, woe to the seagull,
O seagull, poor unhappy bird,
She who wove her nest, laid her eggs,
By the well-trod road.

Where some young travelling merchants,
There did stop to graze their oxen,
And did chase the gull away,
Stole her little children.

The seagull rose and there did circle,
Then down to the road did hurtle,
To the damp, cold earth she falls,
To the men she calls.

'Oh, most kind and noble merchants,
Still so young, no more than children,
Give back my little chickens,
My own little children.'

'No, you shall not ever see them,
Nor fold them close, no, I'll not yield,
For you'll gather them about you,
And fly off to the field.'

'I will never fly away,
I'll stay here, oh, I will stay,
Here to watch over your oxen,
To mind my little children.'

'Fly, unhappy seagull, fly,
To the far green hills, fly,
For your children's necks are broken,
And in my pot they lie.'

'My children's slim necks are broken,
Dead in your pot they lie,
Then may your oxen sicken,
Sicken all and die.

May you know no journey's end,
May your travels last for ever,
For my children are dead,
Lost to me for ever.'

Everyone enjoys MOKRINA's *singing. Especially* ARSEI.
And especially the youngest agitator, YURKO. *He looks at
her with pleasure and interest.* MOKRINA *ends her song,
looking sadly into the distance, as if, at her thirteen years,
she knows something more than the others. Some are
saddened, some sigh,* IVAN IVANYCH *smiles.*

IVAN IVANYCH. So, whose are you, then?

FEODOSII (*with well-rehearsed pride*). Mine, that is. She's the
smartest girl in the class, mine is. She's only thirteen, but she's
already got a few lads after her. Still, I won't be giving her
away in marriage. Not until she's done her learning and grown
up proper.

MOKRINA (*outraged*). Dad!

MOKRINA *runs from the stage, covering her face with
her hands.* YURKO *runs onto the stage and, in order to
change the mood, launches into a jaunty foot-stamping
chechetka.*

The livestock return to the yard: cows, horses, goats and sheep. They are sleek and good to look at. The woman of the house sprinkles salt on bread and feeds her favourite cow.

The shepherd sits at the table and eats his fill after a long day at work.

* * *

A hospital ward. A few terminally ill patients. One corpse. A boy of about fourteen, LYONECHKA, who has lost a leg. A NURSE with a luxuriant bust stands in the doorway.

MORTKO, recovered after an injury, sits in the middle of the ward, putting on his military tunic. He fastens the belt, wraps his puttees around his legs, and pulls high boots on over the top. Then he puts on his army greatcoat, and he places a few parcels in his rucksack. All the PATIENTS *who are able to do so watch him solemnly, with some envy and yet with respect and excitement.* LYONECHKA *makes enormous efforts not to cry, but when* MORTKO *stands, puts on his rucksack, picks up a bundle of books, and walks with a slight limp to the door,* LYONECHKA *can no longer restrain himself and he sobs into his pillow.* MORTKO *hesitates, then returns to* LYONECHKA*'s bed, sits on the edge and takes hold of* LYONECHKA*'s remaining bare foot. He tweaks the toes, and sings a children's song:*

MORTKO (*singing*).
> Old Ma Magpie, making porridge,
> Stirs the pot with broken sticks,

He makes circular movements on LYONECHKA*'s sole.*

> To feed her five magpie chicks.
> For this one a plate – it lit the grate,
> > (*Massages the little toe.*)
> And this one a cup – it washed the pots up,
> > (*Massages the next toe, and so on.*)
> And this one a spoon – it swept all the room,
> And this one a ladle – it laid the bare table,

But this big one here goes hungry today...
For it slipped out the door and slept in the hay.

He tickles LYONECHKA*'s foot.* LYONECHKA *dissolves into laughter and doesn't stop laughing until* MORTKO *has stopped tickling him.*

Yes, you laugh, Lyonechka. A joke or two helps you get through. I mean, look at me – when I was brought in, I was a wreck, I was... Comrades, we must enjoy our jokes. I like a good joke, myself...

TERMINALLY ILL PATIENT. So you've made Soviet citizens of us all. Where are you off to now?

MORTKO. Back to my home country. The Ukraine. I've been reading in the newspaper, in *Pravda,* that the party has achieved a critical breakthrough over there in the development of land use and of our peasants. Agricultural collectivisation is moving on apace and even overtaking heavy industry. This is the beginning of mass collectivisation. If that's the case, then those kulaks will be rising up.

LYONECHKA. Don't go back to those filthy Ukrainians. Come with me to my village, Bryukhovka. My mam is wonderful. Marry her and come and live with us...

MORTKO. And what about your rich neighbour? The one who shot your leg off for stealing an apple from his tree? Is it really so wonderful there?

LYONECHKA. With you, everywhere is wonderful.

MORTKO. I can't, my little one. I've had my orders. You take my ration cards, and I'll be going.

NURSE (*sobbing*). Not even so much as a hug... Stuck in his books the whole time... I'll never, ever forget you.

LYONECHKA. In two years' time I'll be seventeen and then I'm going to be like you. Fighting for the truth. Making people happier.

MORTKO. You be an airman. I always wanted to be an airman.
I've got an airman's soul. Have you heard our song...

(*Singing*.)
> Oh, we were born to make a dream come true,
> To rule the length and breadth of the skies,

LYONECHKA *and then all the others take up the tune and
sing. It is heartfelt.*

ALL (*singing*).
> Our minds have clothed us all in steel,
> And our heart, a motor, flames inside.
>
> So higher and higher and higher,
> We fly like birds in the sky,
> And with every spin of the propeller,
> The peace in our country thrives.

MORTKO *stands and, limping slightly, he leaves. Everyone
falls silent.* MORTKO *can be heard leaving along the
corridor, singing the Soviet Aviation March as he goes.*

MORTKO (*singing*).
> And when we send our plane to the heavens,
> Or when we reach much higher than before,
> We see our Soviet pilots strengthen,
> The first proletarian air force.
>
> So higher and higher and higher,
> We fly like birds in the sky,
> And with every spin of the propeller,
> The peace in our country thrives.
>
> Our eagle eyes unmask every atom,
> Our nerves are steeled, our every judgement sure,
> And they who dare to give us ultimatums,
> Should reckon with our Soviet Air Force.

The NURSE *sits down next to* LYONECHKA. *She looks after*
MORTKO, *crossing herself, but* LYONECHKA *slaps her hand
down. The* NURSE *isn't offended. She presses his head against
her breast in a sudden passion. She grieves for* MORTKO.

12 January 1931

The village reading room. An empty hall with benches and a single bookshelf, on which are newspapers and a few books. People are sitting on the benches. They don't quite know what to do with their hands and so lay them, palms upwards, on their knees. RUDENKO *walks about on the 'stage', holding a copy of* Pravda, *and reading an article aloud.*

RUDENKO *(reading aloud).* 'The party has achieved a critical breakthrough in the development of land use and of the peasantry. The collectivisation programme is moving on apace and even overtaking heavy industry. This is the beginning of mass collectivisation.'

FEODOSII *enters the room last of all. He doesn't sit, but remains standing to one side. He meets* ARSEI's *gaze –* ARSEI *is standing next to him.*

FEODOSII *(quietly).* Don't look at me like I'm some old misery. She's too young to get married. Not sixteen yet. Don't get upset. And anyway. What sort of wife would she make? Or you, husband? You're a pauper. Am I going to give my daughter away to a pauper? You just wait a while and maybe we'll see later on.

ARSEI *turns away indifferently, spits on the floor and wipes the spit away with his foot.*

RUDENKO *(reading aloud).* 'Comrade Stalin informs us that the "most recent and the most decisive change has been in the way that peasants have joined the collectivisation programme – not in ones and twos, but whole villages and districts, even regions." What does this signify? The fact that peasants of middling wealth and standing are entering into collectivisation. This is a major breakthrough in the development of agriculture, and perhaps the highest achievement of the Soviet Government.'

GOROBETS. Who's that, then, they're writing about there?

SAMSON. That's about us, there, that is.

GOROBETS (*admiringly*). Well, those fuckers know how to spin a yarn.

SAMSON. That they do.

RUDENKO. In all my life I've never seen such a stubborn crowd. Will they ever believe? This is *Pravda* here. 'The Truth'!

He shakes the newspaper. The CROWD *has lost interest, they are streaming for the exit. Only the younger ones remain.*

Stop. There's something else… An announcement to make. As you know, Yanik Prokopenko has gone off to build railways. So we need another person on the board of educators. I nominate Arsei Pechoritsa. He's a bright boy. Poor family.

ARSEI. No time.

RUDENKO. Be quiet, you parasite, who's asking you, anyway?

FEODOSII (*kindly*). See, you'll go far, boy. One day I might even be running after you to set you up with Mokrina.

It's clear that FEODOSII *doesn't think this is the least bit likely, and nor does* ARSEI.

RUDENKO. Do we all agree? Is it a unanimous decision?

KILINA. When's the dancing?

RUDENKO. This is a reading hall, not a dance club. Where's your political awareness? All you lot want to do is sing and dance.

The young people are already pushing the benches back to the walls. MOKRINA's *brother* ONIS'KO *draws on his accordion.* KILINA, *a beauty at the height of her looks, goes to the centre of the circle.* RUDENKO, *like many of the*

others, can't take his eyes off her. But she has eyes only for
ARSEI. MOKRINA *stands timidly, wedged in a corner,*
together with the other teenagers.

Put the benches back in their places.

ONIS'KO, *almost as if against his will, plays a cheerful*
tune. KILINA *begins to dance.*

MOKRINA*'s gaze meets* ARSEI*'s. He turns away.*

MOKRINA. I was waiting for you for ages. I'm frozen.

ARSEI. I was behind a tree watching you, wondering whether
you'd wait for me. I thought: 'If she waits, I'll marry her. If
she doesn't, I won't.'

MOKRINA. If I'd known, I'd have run away.

ARSEI. How could you? I wouldn't have let you.

MOKRINA. Don't be so sure of yourself.

ARSEI. Me? I had to have a drink to give me courage.

MOKRINA. And what good will drinking do you?

ARSEI. You know when I first loved you? You couldn't even
walk. I watched you and I thought: 'Sweet little thing. Make
a nice little sister.' And then we both got older and it was
different. It wasn't a little sister I wanted, but a… kiss. And
you, when did you first love me?

MOKRINA (*quietly*). When I first saw you, that's when I first
loved you. I don't remember when. All my life.

ARSEI. Today I will come and ask for your hand, Mokrina.

MOKRINA. Don't. They won't give it. I know for certain.

ARSEI. What about if I spent the night with you? Then they
would.

MOKRINA (*provocatively*). Try it.

ARSEI *nudges against her shoulder and sniffs.*

ARSEI. Would I hurt you like that, my sweetheart?

MOKRINA. Perhaps you will, Arsei.

MOKRINA *strokes* ARSEI*'s head. He lifts it and they kiss.*

But for now ARSEI *dances with* KILINA, *giving* MOKRINA *provocative little glances all the while.*

Easter 1931

A wealthy peasant's house. An OLD MAN *sits at the table. On the table: kulich (Easter bread), Easter eggs and sweet curds, pig fat, bread, soused apples and a bottle of wine. He and his beautiful young companion are eating their Easter breakfast. They each hold an egg in one hand and they are beating them together – the* OLD MAN*'s breaks first and the* WOMAN *laughs, the* OLD MAN *laughs too.*

There is a knock at the door. The OLD MAN *frowns, he makes a signal to the* WOMAN *who covers the table with a towel and pulls a curtain over the icon in the corner.*

MORTKO *enters. He is tired and his limp is more pronounced. He looks carefully at the* OLD MAN, *the* OLD MAN *at him.*

MORTKO (*melting into a smile*). Christ is risen.

OLD MAN (*smiling in relief*). Christ is risen indeed.

MORTKO. Christ is risen.

OLD MAN. Christ is risen indeed.

MORTKO. Christ is risen.

OLD MAN. Christ is risen indeed.

They kiss three times.

Come in, my good man. Sit and eat with us. Have you come far?

MORTKO. From Moscow itself.

MORTKO *eats with appetite*.

OLD MAN (*respectfully*). And how is Moscow? Still standing?

MORTKO. It is.

OLD MAN. Did you see Lenin?

MORTKO. Lenin's dead. Died a good while back.

OLD MAN (*in amazement*). Lenin? But they said he was immortal.

MORTKO. Well, they lied, the red shites.

OLD MAN. Pour our guest a glass, Marfa.

The WOMAN, *looking at* MORTKO *with curiosity, fills his glass*.

So what brings you to Bryukhovka?

MORTKO. Just passing through. Thought I'd pass on regards to you.

OLD MAN. I don't think I know anyone in Moscow. Who is it?

MORTKO. Little boy. Lyonechka.

WOMAN (*crying out*). My son! Is he alive?

OLD MAN. Well, there's a good thing, a good thing.

MORTKO. Lovely apples of yours, these.

WOMAN. They're not mine! I don't own them.

OLD MAN. She's my neighbour. The apples are from my orchard.

WOMAN. So how is my Lyonechka? I thought he was dead!

MORTKO. He's alive. Of course he is. And he'll live. Only one leg, of course.

OLD MAN. Well, that's not so bad. People do manage on one leg.

MORTKO. Really? Why don't you try?

He pushes the table over and shoots the OLD MAN *in both of his legs. The* OLD MAN *falls down in shock. The* WOMAN *shrieks and falls to* MORTKO'*s feet.*

WOMAN. I was hungry… What was I supposed to do? You won't kill me, will you? You're my saviour, not my murderer! You've come to save me, not to kill me!

She looks at MORTKO *with hope.* MORTKO *hesitates, thinking.*

* * *

Spring. Birds twittering. Snow melting. The square in front of the church with the village hall nearby. A CROWD *stands in front of the church and watches* ARSEI, *who has climbed up the bell tower with a rope in his hands.*

ODARKA. Son, what you doing up there?

KILINA. Are you looking for Moscow?

ARSEI. Aye, and what else would I be doing up here?

ODARKA. Come down, you bloody fool, you'll kill yourself!

ARSEI. Arsei Pechoritsa, pauper and bloody fool, is making his stand. We've had enough of your God messing us around.

NEIGHBOUR. What's your Arsei on about? Young people and their tricks, is it? Where's the priest? It's time for mass.

RUDENKO. Open your eyes! We are liberating you! Do you need a hand with the bell, Arsei?

ARSEI. Do it myself.

RUDENKO. Well then, get on with it and stop speechifying!

ARSEI (*to* FEODOSII, *provoking him*). Eh, Feodosii, you, won't you stop me sinning?

FEODOSII. What are you up to? Are you going to jump? (*Calmly, to* MOKRINA.) Daughter, why don't you tell that idiot to come down off there.

MOKRINA. You think he'd listen?

ARSEI. So then, Feodosii, sir... are you going to give over your Mokrina to me?

ODARKA (*trembling, to* FEODOSII). Just say it, man, tell him that you will... And when he gets down I'll throttle him with my own two hands... (*To* ARSEI.) Why do you want this Mokrina, son? They'll begrudge you a crust of bread, that family will. You take Kilina, she's one of us, she loves you...

KILINA. Stop that, eh?

ARSEI. So then, Feodosii, will you give her to me?

FEODOSII. Course I will, son. Just as soon as you get down, we'll have a big wedding.

MOKRINA (*quietly*). I'm not marrying a fool.

FEODOSII. He's no fool, that boy. I can see that.

ONIS'KO. Arsei, what are you doing up there? Is that how you find your brides?

MOKRINA. Arsei, are you drunk?

ARSEI. Say you love me.

Laughter in the CROWD.

ODARKA. His dad was another one.

MOKRINA. I love you, for God's sake, is that any way to disgrace me in front of people?

KILINA. Oh, she loves him, does she? If he was doing it for me... I'd have flown up that tower.

RUDENKO. Pechoritsa, I'll give you three days in the lock-up for ruining the whole concept...

A TRAMP *approaches – a thin, grey-haired wanderer.*

TRAMP. Christ is risen, friends.

CROWD. Christ is risen indeed.

TRAMP. What is going on?

GAFIIKA. See that Arsei man? – Well, he's climbed up the bells and he wants to jump – (*With pride.*) and it's over my sister.

TRAMP (*crossing himself*). On this day? Lord forgive him. Come down, boy. Today is Easter Day. And you have your whole life before you.

SAMSON. D'you remember how my Galia, your Godmother, gave you an Easter cake and some painted eggs? She'd be turning in her grave, the darling, if she could see you now.

They all look at RUDENKO *without sympathy.* ARSEI *goes to the edge.*

MOKRINA (*who has lost all sense of shame*). I love you, Arsei, I love you! Come down, sweetheart!

ARSEI. Be quiet. No need to disgrace yourself. Should have thought of that earlier.

RUDENKO. Would you listen to the fucker! He was sent up there by order of the Soviet Government, and now he's up there solving all his kulak personal problems. Get working up there, Pechoritsa! Or I'll try declaring my love for you, too!

GOROBETS. Well, I drowned myself in the River Khorol over a woman. But then I knew how to swim. I don't remember Arsei up there ever doing much flying.

The CROWD *laughs.* ARSEI *makes his way determinedly towards the bell. And there, sitting on the crossbeam, he begins tying his rope to the bell.*

There is a bewildered murmuring in the CROWD.

RUDENKO (*joyfully*). In the name of Soviet power, we rid the people of their religious oppression. The church will become a grain store! The bells will be melted down for the use of the State!

From far off, something black, rolling down the hill towards the church, can be seen. It transforms itself from a small black crow into a fat priest in flowing robes. He runs, stumbling, falls, lifts his hands to the heavens. But nobody sees him. Everyone is watching ARSEI, as if entranced. Nobody laughs any more and nobody speaks. They breathe, gulping at the air.

ARSEI *ties the rope fast and now he carries the bell on the rope out of the bell tower.*

TRAMP. Fight back! Right now. Why are you standing watching, good people?

WOMAN. What is he up to? I don't understand…

MAN. That bell's going to fall.

WOMAN. Or is he doing it on purpose? I just don't understand…

The TRAMP *goes up to each in turn, looking in their faces.*

TRAMP. Fight back, there's no time. Where I come from, near Gadyach, it's already begun… The Devil came and took everything away… We're starving… Dying like flies.

ODARKA *makes the sign of the cross on* ARSEI *from a distance with a small gesture.*

ODARKA. Lord forgive him, Lord forgive him, he won't drop it. He'll have his fun, but he won't drop it. It won't happen.

ARSEI *drags the bell to the edge.*

ARSEI. Move away, or someone will get hurt.

RUDENKO (*grandly*). Remember this moment, comrades. From this moment your new life begins. You haven't realised the full importance of this moment because of your

ignorance. But we are opening the people's eyes for them.
Tonight, everyone should attend a lecture in the reading hall
on approaches to strengthening the anti-religious movement.
Hey, come on, then, Arsei, lad!

Down with all the priests,
The rabbis, monks and nuns,
We'll climb up to the heavens,
Those gods have had their fun!

The CROWD *scatters like mice, stopping a little way off.*
ARSEI *lowers the bell on the rope, but halfway down the
bell comes free of the rope and falls, breaking with a
moaning clang into several pieces.*

The people in the CROWD *weep and cross themselves.*

MOKRINA. What a fool I've found myself, Arsei... Didn't you
think... Where are we to be wed...?

May 1931

MOKRINA *and* ARSEI, *both in their best clothes, leave the
village party administration building.* ARSEI *is triumphant,
excited and happy.* MOKRINA *is wearing a foolish smile.*

ARSEI. Now we're husband and wife. Do you realise? And
your dad can't say anything.

MOKRINA. Oh, he can. And he will. We'll get a tongue-
lashing.

ARSEI. I'm not afraid of that. It's lawful, can't be taken back,
and that's what matters. What are you laughing about?

MOKRINA *covers her mouth with her hands to stop herself
bursting into laughter.* ARSEI *smiles too, looking at her.*

My giggling girl. What?

MOKRINA. Oh, stop it, Arsei… What sort of wife do I make?

ARSEI. My lawful wife. Look, it's here, written down. We were registered by the village Soviet. You new name is Mokrina Pechoritsa, Arsei's wife. What's wrong?

MOKRINA. No. I don't feel it. Don't show that bit of paper to anyone. They'll laugh.

ARSEI (*confused*). Everyone gets registered now.

MOKRINA. Well, I don't believe in it. I have been to weddings, you know. My sister was married, in a church. It was beautiful.

ARSEI. But only after being registered by the village Soviet.

MOKRINA. All right, and now we've been registered we can get married properly –

I'd like that.

ARSEI. I'm not allowed. You know I'm not. Why did you do it, then? Why did you agree? You're just messing me around.

MOKRINA. I thought something would happen, that it would change things. That I'd feel different. But nothing. I just feel ashamed, like when I was a child. And that's it.

ARSEI. Come home. Mum has been baking cakes.

MOKRINA. I'm going home. To my home. Sorry, Arsei. That wasn't it. And let's not tell anyone…

ARSEI (*exploding*). You bitch, Mokrina! You bitch! I'll make you sorry for this!

MOKRINA. Don't be angry.

ARSEI. It's your dad! All his doing! He doesn't realise that I'll be rich soon.

MOKRINA. But why are you poor? I'm not afraid of being poor. But people say that your dad was given everything by the Soviet in 1919 – land and credit, and now you're poor again. Why is that? My dad says it's because you'll only work to a master. Is that true?

ARSEI. We'll see, in a year's time, who's poor and who works to a master. Silly fool. Your only hope is to marry me. You kulaks will be destroyed soon, and then you'll come begging bread off me.

MOKRINA. And you won't give me any?

ARSEI. I wouldn't let you through the door.

MOKRINA *laughs*.

MOKRINA. We'll get married in church. One day.

An OLD WOMAN *holding an empty bucket passes by.*

Good day to you.

OLD WOMAN. And to you, child.

ARSEI. Good day.

OLD WOMAN (*to* ARSEI). Get out of my way.

OLD WOMAN *gives* ARSEI *a hostile look and tries to pass him quickly.*

ARSEI. Why's that old witch looking at me like that?

MOKRINA. Because people don't like you any more.

ARSEI. I don't understand. I'd do anything for you. You want a church wedding? Let's go to Sorochintsy. And they can put me in prison for it. And my mother can die of hunger. Is that what you want? I'd do anything for you.

MOKRINA. There's no need for that.

ARSEI. Well, what do you want, then?

MOKRINA. The right thing.

ARSEI (*enraged*). Oh, 'the right thing'! Go back to your fucking family, you kulak bitch!

He pushes MOKRINA *in the chest. She falls against the fence. He turns and leaves. The* OLD WOMAN *with an empty bucket passes him as he walks away. She goes to*

MOKRINA *and helps her stand.* MOKRINA, *crying, watches* ARSEI *walk away.*

OLD WOMAN. I had a dream that your Arsei came to my house and ate all my dumplings. And today Artyukh told me that Arsei has been enlisted as an activist with the rest of the wastrels. They'll be round confiscating goods from everyone and keeping back twenty-five per cent for themselves. There, see.... So don't you go crying for him, child.

MORTKO *enters in a dusty greatcoat. He is limping. He smiles warmly.*

MORTKO. Where's the party administration?

MOKRINA. Over there.

MORTKO. I've come a long way... I like it here...

OLD WOMAN. What brings you here, then, soldier?

MORTKO. I've been sent here. I was sent to you. Here I am.

He smiles. MOKRINA *smiles shyly back, and runs away, her face still tear-stained.*

OLD WOMAN (*looking closely at* MORTKO). Your face looks familiar. Did I dream of you, was that it?

21 November 1932

The STARITSKII FAMILY *are at the table, eating. It is a large family. Eleven children and the mother and father.*

There is a lot of boiled potato, pickled cabbage, pig fat, bread. They eat silently and heartily, with wooden spoons from shared dishes. The CHILDREN *whisper and giggle, but fall silent under the stern gaze of their father,* FEODOSII.

FEODOSII. Good borshch, Oliana. Only not quite enough vinegar.

OLIANA. Well, the pickled beetroot is finished.

FEODOSII (*raising his eyebrows, startled*). What do you mean, 'finished'? Oliana, what's got into you? How could that happen?

OLIANA *shrugs, surprised – hardly understanding herself how something like that could happen. They eat for a while longer in silence and then* FEODOSII *puts his spoon aside.*

I don't understand it. I've lived a good long life, but I've never eaten borshch without pickled beetroot. I've known the bread run out. The potatoes. But pickled beetroot?!

OLIANA. I don't know. I pickled enough for the whole winter... but I looked today and the barrel's nearly empty... Nothing like that's ever happened before... And the cabbage is almost finished.

MOKRINA. We'll survive without beetroot, Dad.

FEODOSII. Hmm. First we'll survive without beetroot, and then without bread. And then we'll survive without a god. Fine people we'll be after all that. What will be left of us?

There is a loud knocking at the door.

Who's there?

The door opens. The AGITATORS *stand on the threshold.*

The frightened FAMILY *stand up together, leave the table and line up against the wall. The other* PEASANTS *join them.*

The AGITATORS *are giving a concert to the silent* CROWD.

Each peasant holds an empty bowl and a wooden spoon.

IVAN IVANYCH.
Last-but-one show for the poor deceived peasants!
A visual aid for the aiders of the kulaks!

(*Announces.*) Scene Number One: 'Mr Kulak refuses to join the collective farm.'

MASHA *and* VASILII *sit at the table, dressed in a caricature of Ukrainian peasant dress. MASHA is wearing a brightly embroidered shirt and a bonnet on her head. She has stuffed something up the shirt to increase her bust. Next to her, VASILII is wearing a fake moustache and a Ukrainian 'topknot' on his head. They look nothing like any of the actual peasants who are standing and watching. On the table there is a pretend roast suckling pig and a round loaf and dumplings.*

YURKO *enters, dressed as a poor Komsomolets. He has a warm friendly smile on his face.*

YURKO. Good day, kind people!

MASHA *and* VASILII (*unwelcoming*). Hello.

YURKO. In the name of the Soviet State, I invite you to join the collective farm.

MASHA. Don't want to.

YURKO. Why?

VASILII. We don't want to work for the State. We want to work for ourselves.

YURKO. It will be better for everyone in the collective farm.

MASHA. Well, we don't want it to be better for everyone. We want it to be good for us.

YURKO (*pointing an accusing finger at them*). You're kulak individualists!

The CROWD *gasps.* MASHA *and* VASILII *shrink in terror and hate.*

IVAN IVANYCH. Scene Two: 'Mr Kulak refuses to give up his bread and property to the State.'

MASHA *and* VASILII *hide all the pretend food in the stove. They sit down at an empty table.* YURKO *enters.* MASHA *and* VASILII *look at him in rage.*

YURKO. Good day to you all.

MASHA *and* VASILII *are silent.*

The Soviet State is asking for your help.

VASILII. We haven't got anything.

YURKO. What do you mean? What about bread? Give up your spare bread to the State.

MASHA. We haven't got any spare bread.

YURKO. Hand your horses, cows and pigs over to the collective farm.

VASILII. The cows have got scab, the pigs have got a fungus, and our horses are all sick old nags. Go away. You won't get anything from us.

YURKO (*leaving, with pain*).
    We asked you very nicely,
    We came to you in trust,
    But you turned your fleshy kulak backs,
    And showed your fists to us.

    YURKO *leaves.*

IVAN IVANYCH. Scene Number Three: 'The Communist activists confiscate the kulaks' hidden bread, which has been stolen from the State.'

    YURKO *enters, together with* ARSEI, GAVRILO *and* YUKHIM. MASHA *and* VASILII *huddle in fear against the wall, together with the watching* CROWD.

YURKO. Give the bread back to the State.

MASHA. There isn't any, you fool. How will I feed the children?

YURKO. So what's this, then?

He reaches into the stove and begins pulling loaf after loaf after loaf from it, like a magician, and handing them to the others: ARSEI, GAVRILO *and* YUKHIM.

OLIANA (*calling in desperation from the* CROWD). Wretches! How will she feed the children?

ARSEI. And what's this?

He takes out a pole with a sharp metal point on it and begins poking at the walls, floor and ceiling. Grain comes pouring out. There is the bellowing of frightened, rounded-up livestock outside. Pigs squeal.

YUKHIM *opens a trunk and stands stock-still for a second, amazed at its contents. He pulls beautiful scarves, embroidered fabrics, linen shirts from the trunk, and* ARSEI *takes them from him.*

The AGITATORS *bring various other peasants into the scene (not all of them), taking from them their scarves, their boots, their jackets and overcoats. The peasants offer them up willingly, like participants in a magic show. Some resist timidly: the* OLD WOMAN *with the empty bucket doesn't want to give the bucket up, but the* AGITATORS *take it. They spend a particularly long time pulling the boots off an* OLD MAN… *He kicks and swears and spits and curses.*

OLD MAN. Will you fuck off, you fucking shites, fuck off and die, the lot of you. You're not having the boots off me! You can burn in hell, for all I care! May the little devils run off with you, and your kids never know a pair of shoes or a day's happiness!

He is dragged off the stage together with his boots. MASHA *and* VASILII, *coming out of their 'roles', collect up all the confiscated goods and carry them off.*

There is silence. YURKO *steps back.*

MASHA *and* VASILII *are no longer visible.*

Only IVAN IVANYCH *is in his place.*

IVAN IVANYCH. The confiscated goods will be sold to the poor for next to nothing. Surely after all these years of poverty and injustice they deserve to wear fine linen and boots made of pigskin?

After this rhetorical question, IVAN IVANYCH *leaves the scene.*

A cart rolls in. Piled high upon it are real household goods and clothes: not just the best clothing, but clothes for every day, and bowls, barrels, pots, buckets, yokes...

MORTKO *and* ARSEI *enter, but* ARSEI *is not instantly recognisable: he is wearing a greatcoat, like* MORTKO*'s, and a leather cap. He is slightly embarrassed, but at the same time he struts and preens.*

MORTKO (*benignly*). Surely after all these years of poverty and injustice, you deserve to wear fine clothes?

ARSEI. I've dreamed of wearing a coat like this since I was a child.

MORTKO. Dreams come true, Arsei. And the poor in your village have been dreaming just like you. So make their dreams come true... If they can't afford to buy anything, then give them the kulaks' possessions for free. And people will speak highly of you. Girls will come running.

ARSEI. They do anyway. Just not the right ones.

MORTKO. That's because you're choosing the wrong ones.

ARSEI. She's a kulak. A collectivised kulak.

MORTKO. Well then, she's just like everyone else now. She'll make you a good wife.

ARSEI. Oh, I'm not so sure.

MORTKO. She will. You just wait and see. You'll finish your studies at the party school and come back an important man... She won't be able to take her eyes off you.

He claps ARSEI *on the shoulder encouragingly. The* VILLAGERS *are returning to the square.* MOKRINA *and* ONIS'KO *lead the suddenly much-aged* FEODOSII *by the arm. He stands there, leaning on his eldest children.* MORTKO *smiles approvingly at* ARSEI.

Go on, then. Like I taught you. You'll be fine once you're started.

ARSEI goes uncertainly towards the cart. The VILLAGERS *look at him sullenly.* MORTKO *stands to one side and watches.*

ARSEI (*timidly*). Good morning, everyone… What a lovely day, eh? Sun's out…

They are all silent. They watch ARSEI. ARSEI *looks back at* MORTKO *uncertainly.* MORTKO *smiles encouragingly.*

(*Uncertain at first but becoming bolder and bolder.*) And who cares about the sun, when there's a whole cartload of presents for you all here. Come on, then, all of you, come closer. Let me tell you what this is about… We're going to hand out the kulaks' wealth to the poor… Sell it to you for next to nothing.

SAMSON. What's that about, then? Seize all our goods, and then hand it all back to us? Why did you take it in the first place? Mighty clever of you.

GOROBETS. So I'm going to be walking round in my neighbour's coat whilst he freezes to death? Is that it? We're hardly going to be on speaking terms.

ODARKA. Haven't we done our stint of freezing to death? Let them freeze. Try out how it feels to be us, and we can see what it feels like to be them.

ARSEI lifts a jacket off the heap of clothes.

ARSEI. There's a jacket for you.

ARTYUKH. That's Feodosii's jacket.

ARSEI. And it's a lovely jacket, isn't it? Feodosii paid no less than ten roubles for that, but I'll give it to you for two. What a giveaway.

FEODOSII. And what will you spend the money on?

ARSEI. We'll give the money to the State and the State will use it to feed orphans.

SAMOILENKO. I'll have the jacket, then. Do my bit for the orphans. Don't mind, do you, Feodosii? You won't hold it against me?

FEODOSII. May God be your judge.

SAMOILENKO. God's been abolished, hasn't he? And I've always wanted a jacket like yours. Embroidered, and with gilded buttons. Come on, all of you, don't be shy. Don't want to spend our whole lives in wretched poverty, do we?

She goes over to ARSEI *and gives him two roubles. She puts the jacket on and looks pleased with herself.*

VOICE. No shame.

ARSEI. And look at this pot. Not one of the ordinary old pots we make our soup in. Oh no – this one is decorated and it comes all the way from Kiev itself. Look, it says 'Kiev' here. Twenty kopecks.

ARTYUKH. That was Mark's pot when he was still alive.

KILINA. Leave it be! The poor man was dying and he had nothing to drink water from.

GAVRILO. But he had somewhere to shit. In his trousers.

GAVRILO *bursts into stupid laughter, but no one else joins him.* ARSEI *puts the pot down and lifts up a woman's shift.*

ARSEI. You don't want the pot? Well, have this shift, then. Pure white linen. Sort of thing only a fat-cat landowner would wear... In shirts like these they'd have been rolling about in their feather beds whilst we were breaking our backs in their fields. I'm giving it away. Who wants it? Kilina, do you want it? You can have it for free.

KILINA. I don't want Mokrina's shift.

ARSEI (*confused and embarrassed*). Is it yours, then? Take it, sweetheart...

But MOKRINA *is holding her father up.* MORTKO *makes a warning gesture to* ARSEI.

Well, I won't give it to you. It's not meant for you kulaks, all this.

WOMAN. I'll have it. Not for myself. For my daughter. She's ill... Give her something to be pleased about.

She takes the shirt and tries not to look into anyone's eyes. She leaves. ARSEI *takes some thin linen 'bloomers' with lacy edges from the heap. There is laughter.* MOKRINA, *recognising them as hers, covers her face with her hands in shame.*

ARSEI (*laughing*). And what's this wondrous object?

GAVRILO. Ah, that's Mokrina's undergarments, that is. Didn't you recognise them?

ARSEI. Well, I've not seen them yet. So how come you recognised them, you dirty little shit? Or do you need a beating to teach you to keep your tongue to yourself?

GAVRILO. It's just she's gone as red as a lobster. Aren't you wearing anything under your skirt, Mokrina? Let's have a look!

ONIS'KO. You piece of cheap meat! I'll rip your balls off to pay you back for that, for my sister.

ONIS'KO, *leaving* MOKRINA *supporting* FEODOSII, *comes out for a fight with* GAVRILO, *who instantly takes to his heels, teasing* ONIS'KO *as he runs away with silly rhymes.*

GAVRILO. Onis'ko, Onis'ko... Where does all his piss go...

MOKRINA. Oh, leave him. Don't pay any attention. Gavrilo always teases everyone. It's not worth it.

ARSEI. I'll have a word with him afterwards. He won't tease you again, Mokrina.

MOKRINA. Give me back my scarf, Arsei. I've nothing to cover my head with. Didn't you come courting me once? This is all my dowry piled up here.

ARSEI. I'll take you without a dowry. I don't want anything else apart from you. When I get back from the party school, will you marry me?

ONIS'KO. She wouldn't even shit in the same place as you, you pauper scum.

ARSEI. You useless fucker. I could save your family from Siberia, and there you are, still going on about my poverty.

ONIS'KO. And how many times have we saved your family, have you forgotten that? When your wheat failed, or when your drunken father fell in the ditch and froze. What has happened to you, Arsei? You've changed. We grew up together, remember how we used to go down trading at the bazaar together, how we spent nights together grazing the horses out in the fields... And now you're attacking us... stealing from your brothers, and you're not even embarrassed to do it, you're pleased with yourself... Good people, you're like a herd of cattle, just standing there, watching. Take sticks, take fire, and we'll defend our goods, our lives, and our families! Or men like Arsei will be walking around in our clothes and enjoying our sisters...!

The CROWD *become agitated and noisy.*

ARSEI. I'll shut you up, you kulak shit!

ARSEI *throws himself at* ONIS'KO *and tries to hit him, but he gets caught up in the folds of his huge greatcoat and trips. Everyone laughs.* MOKRINA, *gasping, lets go of* FEODOSII *and rushes forward to* ARSEI *to help him stand.*

MORTKO *lifts his gun and points it at* ONIS'KO.

FEODOSII, *left without any support, falls to the ground.*

All of a sudden the radio sounds loudly on the square. Everyone is frozen to the spot, they listen. MORTKO *still aims at* ONIS'KO. *An ancient horror spreads over the faces in the* CROWD.

RADIO. The party, under Stalin's leadership, has imposed special measures against the kulaks and has broken their resistance. Those causing harm have been severely punished. Comrade Stalin has asked the party to learn lessons from this and called on Bolshevik farmers to become technical experts and develop a new cadre of technical workers from the proletariat and the rural classes.

ARSEI *stops* MOKRINA, *takes his bundle of possessions and leaves*. YUKHIM *and* GAVRILO *leave with him*.

MOKRINA *and* KILINA *wave a handkerchief in farewell to the young men walking away*.

MOKRINA *and* KILINA (*chanting*).
Oh, where, my fine lad, are you going to?
On your path, on your road, on your way,
Just a night longer, oh, boy of mine,
Just a night longer, please stay.

IVAN IVANYCH. Scene Four: 'Suppressing the resistance to collectivisation.'

MORTKO (*without lowering his gun*). Staritskii Onis'ko, Mel'nik Kilina, Shevchuk Sekleta, Staritskii Feodosii, Prisiazhniuk Oleksa, Pastukh Pavlo, Gavriliuk Motria.

For resisting collectivisation. In the name of Soviet power. Leave the stage.

All those named take a step forward. They are all wholesome, handsome men and women. Amongst them, MOKRINA's brother and father. Amongst them, KILINA.

The enemies of collectivisation leave the stage to the sound of gunfire.

IVAN IVANYCH. The Fifth and Final Scene: 'The true face of the kulak.'

The working classes slave away in factories, Soviet young people are tirelessly building railways and dams. And what are the Ukrainian kulaks doing? Stealing each other's last piece of grain, leading away the last of the livestock, grazing on the fat of the land like cattle. Looting and cannibalism are on the rise.

There is hardly anyone left. OLIANA, MOKRINA *and some others are either sleeping or sitting with closed eyes, leaning against the fence.*

OLIANA *is sitting by her young son* TODOS. *She is telling him a story.* TODOS *pours water into his bowl. He eats it with a small spoon and murmurs in fatigue.*

A puppet theatre appears from behind the stove. OLIANA *reads the part of the narrator.* TODOS *watches, entranced.*

OLIANA. So Ivasik-Telesik grew to be a man and he asked his father to make him a boat of silver with a golden oar, and he said he would catch fish enough to feed them. So his father made him a boat and put it on the lake, and Ivasik-Telesik sailed about the lake and caught fish for his mother and father. And every day his mother brought him food and she would call him: 'Telesik, Telesik, sail over to the shore, I've brought you food and drink!'

But a hungry snake wanted to eat Telesik. And the snake had her voice forged thin and light by the blacksmith, so it was like Telesik's mother's. Then the snake went to the water's edge and called: 'Telesik, Telesik, sail over to the shore, I've brought you food and drink…'

Telesik heard his mother's voice and sailed to the shore, and the snake caught him and carried him back to her hut, and ordered her daughter Ulianka to cook Telesik for supper. Then the snake went out and Ulianka said to Telesik: 'Jump into the pan!' But Telesik replied: 'I don't know how to. Why don't you show me?'

Ulianka slithered into the pan to show Telesik, and quick as a flash Telesik put her into the oven and cooked her. And then he hid himself. The mother snake came back in the evening and there was cooked meat in the oven. She was just tucking into the meat, when suddenly she heard a voice: 'Fee-fi-fo-fum, that's your daughter's flesh in your tum – '

TODOS *loses interest in the story and the puppets and takes up his mournful howl of lament:*

TODOS. I want to eat.

And he eats the water out of the bowl as if it were soup.

And he weeps. OLIANA *stares helplessly.*

Suddenly a WOMAN *calls* TODOS *from a far corner in a pleasant, high voice.*

SAMOILENKO. Todos, Todos, come over here, I've got food and drink for you… I've got beetroots and carrots and hedgehog and pastry, and meat from a dead horse…

TODOS *gets up and follows the voice, together with his bowl and spoon.* OLIANA *wants to call her son, but can't find the strength to move or even make a sound.* SAMOILENKO *wraps* TODOS *lovingly in her sheepskin and leads him away.*

IVAN IVANYCH. So there we are, comrades, we'll wipe out the last of the kulak plague! A bright new future awaits us! Hurray!

> Keep the flag flying, men!
> And tighten your belts a notch or two!
> There will be no more mercy for the kulak adversary,
> A Soviet sun lifts into view!

To the sounds of life-affirming Soviet music, MASHA, VASILII *and* YURKO *come running back onstage. They are dressed in simple, bright clothes, they shine with joy and happiness. They perform a victory dance.*

24 March 1933

ARSEI *stands bewildered in the reading hall.*

He looks at MORTKO, *who is weeping bitterly at his table.*

On the table lie his rations: bread, pig fat and salt. A pile of books.

Something moves indistinctly in the other corner.

ARSEI. What has happened to you, Mortko? You've changed. Stop it. I've come back to help you.

MORTKO. You've come back… That's good, boy… Because I despair… (*Pointing to the moving heap in the corner.*) Are these people? Is this what we're supposed to be building Communism out of? They nearly ate me alive. Wasters! Parasites! Whole fucking nation of them! They don't want to work. They'll work for a lord and master, but not for each other. Miserable bastards! Where's the bread? Come on, bring me the bread, and look sharp about it! They've hidden it all! Eaten the whole damn lot!

ARSEI. Have you heard anything of Mokrina Staritskaya? What's happened to her?

MORTKO. Dead. Caught a cold and died last week.

ARSEI. Dead?! But I asked you to look –

MORTKO. Ate some bad horsemeat and died.

ARSEI. Are you sure?

MORTKO. No, that's not it. Put on a cart with the corpses and carried away and buried alive in a mass grave.

ARSEI. Mortko?!

MORTKO. Ha! Yes, that's it. Eaten by a cannibal. Samoilenko the Flesheater. Neighbour of yours. What are you looking at me like that for? Your Mokrina married the son of the party representative. Now she's stuffing her face with government rations. You should see the rations he gets! Meat and fish and butter and white bread...

ARSEI *looks dazedly at* MORTKO. *There is a groan from the corner.*

Drowned in the river. They pulled her body out downstream.

He laughs maniacally. And then abruptly stops. Thinks.

Mokrina-Mokrina-Mokrina... (*To the corner.*) Who's this Mokrina, anyone remember?

To ARSEI's *horror, a human figure rises from the moving heap. It pushes in front of itself an object of some sort. The rags on this object move, but it can't walk. It falls to* ARSEI's *feet.* ARSEI *steps back in revulsion.*

ARSEI. What's this?

HUMAN FIGURE. Mokrina.

ARSEI *stares at it. At last he recognises her features. He presses the indifferent* MOKRINA *to his breast.*

ARSEI. Mokrina... my child... alive...

He tears her from his breast and examines her. He catches fleas from her face, clothes and hair. They jump around him, too.

He unties his sack and takes out bread. MOKRINA's *indifference is transformed into greedy interest.* ARSEI *gives her bread. There is a wailing from the corner.* HUMAN SHAPES *crawl rapidly across to* ARSEI, *stretching out their hands.* ARSEI *gives each a piece of bread.*

MORTKO *watches this scene with a strange calm.*

MORTKO. That's right. Help, that's what. That's right, Arsei. You help people. Let them see the new regime is better than the old one.

He picks up his rations and leaves.

MOKRINA *swallows her bread. Now she kisses* ARSEI's *feet.* ARSEI *lifts her from the ground.*

ARSEI. It's all over. You're going to live, Mokrina. You're going to live, my love. I'll see to it.

MOKRINA *reaches into the bag. But* ARSEI *gathers it up.*

That's enough, you'll be ill. You can't have any more. Be patient.

MOKRINA *bellows and bites* ARSEI. *He gently pushes her away.*

(*Laughing.*) Silly love. Don't bite me.

15 April 1933

There is a full moon tonight. Two young ACTIVISTS *are sleeping sweetly with their rifles under the cherry tree by the old church. It has become a grain store: there is no longer a cross on the cupola of the church, nor a bell in the bell tower. The windows are boarded up securely and there is a huge lock on the door.* GOROBETS *and* SAMSON *creep up quietly. They are holding empty sacks.*

GOROBETS (*nodding at the guards*). They won't wake?

SAMSON. I left them half a litre. They're sleeping like babies.

They stop at the bottom end of the church and knock the boards off a small, low window with a crowbar.

GOROBETS (*fondly addressing the window*). My own little window. If it wasn't for you, I'd be pushing up the cemetery daisies by now. (*Remembering something unpleasant.*) Only you know what... I can't go in there this time. It's your turn.

SAMSON. Look at me. I'm not going to fit through there. What's wrong? Scared of mice? Or is it the dark?

GOROBETS (*making each word distinct*). I'm not scared of mice. But when they were running all over me last time, all over my hands and my face... I was... well, I... didn't feel quite right. I almost shouted out.

SAMSON. You're like a girl, Gorobets. Who's scared of mice these days?

GOROBETS. You can say what you like.

SAMSON. But I won't fit through, Gorobets! We had an agreement – you go in for the grain, and I'll stand guard.

GOROBETS (*whining*). I've got no rights... It's just you, you, you... It stinks of mould in there, it's as dark as inside an arse, you use your hand to scoop up the grain and it's all shivering with little mice... If you light a match they all skitter off and watch you with their cursed little eyes from the corners... I'd prefer to die of hunger... I'm not going, Samson.

SAMSON. Maybe you need a little glass of something strong, like last time?

GOROBETS. Last time I saw a little demon. With long whiskers. I'm not going in.

SAMSON. And I was hoping to cook us some gruel. Oh, well... We wasted that half-litre on those shits, then. And your sister at home, hungry...

GOROBETS (*struggles with himself*). All right, then. One last time. You guard me.

Sighing heavily, GOROBETS *crosses himself and climbs in through the window.* SAMSON *holds him. He disappears for a while.* SAMSON *hides in the shadow. There is quiet. All of a sudden* GOROBETS *climbs back out. His sack is empty.* SAMSON *emerges from the shadow.*

SAMSON. The sack's empty.

GOROBETS (*sniffs, then after a pause*). I'm not scared of mice.

SAMSON *spits angrily. He takes the bag from* GOROBETS.

(*Guiltily ingratiating.*) You might fit through now. Bugger me if you're not thinner than you were.

SAMSON. Let's see, eh? If you hear anything, whistle like a nightingale.

GOROBETS *imitates the nightingale's trilling song.*

That's it.

SAMSON *stands undecided in front of the narrow opening.*

GOROBETS. Dive in with your hands and head first, like this. Once your shoulders are in, the rest I can push through.

SAMSON *does as* GOROBETS *tells him. His arms, head and shoulders, with some effort, fit through, but his backside gets stuck.*

That's my boy... There we go...

GOROBETS *busies himself around* SAMSON's *rear end, pushing it in. But in vain.*

Push, Samson, come on now... Wedge your arms against something... hold on... give it some welly...

SAMSON *bellows.* GOROBETS *tires of pushing. He becomes angry.*

Bloody stuffing your belly, you fat pig, that's what it is... Nothing left of the rest of us, but you, you great lardball, you've been puffing out like a pig in clover...

Where the bloody hell did you come from, eh? The rest of us, dying of hunger, bellies swelling, drying out – and nothing happens to you! You can pop with the eating for all I care, fat-chops! Great fat fucker! Will you try and push yourself in!

He kicks SAMSON's *backside a few times and calms down a little.*

Fucking successful grain trip that was… Pull him back out, I s'pose…

He pulls SAMSON*'s legs, but* SAMSON *is stuck fast and won't come out.* GOROBETS *becomes more and more anxious.*

Samson, me boy, give it your best effort this way or that way or we'll be here tomorrow morning. Go on, Samson, I'm begging you…

Nothing. A prolonged fart issues from SAMSON*'s bowels.*

Phwoah… bastard! (*Tries to scare him.*) Hey, Samson, I can hear someone coming!

He trills like a nightingale. SAMSON*'s legs begin wheeling round as if he were riding a bike.*

(*In joyful relief.*) He moved! Thank the Lord! Just don't shit your pants. (*He listens fearfully.*) Oh… someone's definitely coming… Oh Christ, it's the activists, coming home after their meeting… Bloody devils themselves… Well, we're done for… God help us! Samson!

He trills again in desperation. Then he tugs at SAMSON*'s legs. He falls down, powerless, realising that it is all up with them. He cries.*

I'm sorry… Keep as still as death… don't move a muscle…

He takes to his heels and disappears into the bushes.

ARSEI *and* MORTKO *appear.*

ARSEI. Look, Mortko… Beautiful night like this, the nightingales full of song… And we're in there, talking away till dawn and noticing nothing…

MORTKO (*suspiciously*). Bit early for nightingales, Pechoritsa.

ARSEI (*dreamily*). It might be a bit early up in the north where you come from, but we have an early spring and the nightingales… When I used to walk out with my girl, all the nightingales were in song. Will those nights ever come again?

MORTKO. What are you thinking about, eh? You, my fellow, you need to realise that when you go dreaming about the nights you spend with your girl, you're forgetting all about the days. Difficult days, days locked in combat with the enemy. Where's the bloody guard, that's what I want to know…?

He whistles. Silence. He looks about and sees the sleeping GUARDS.

(*Benignly.*) Just look at those wasters, eh? Snoring away. Good thing we came this way.

He goes over to the two GUARDS *and kicks them.*

Drunk as my arse! Fuckers! And you on about nightingales!

He kicks them with his boot, and shakes them. One of them shows some signs of life. His eyes open with an effort – and he sees MORTKO. *He bellows in fear and tries to stand, but falls back down.*

(*Benignly.*) What are we going to do with them? Shoot them on the spot? Summary justice?

ARSEI (*laughs*). It's Gavrilo and Yukhim… What can you do, eh? I've known them since I was a kid. They'd jump off the bell tower for a drop of vodka.

MORTKO. Well, they've jumped too far this time… Bring some water from the well, eh, Arsei? We'll wake them up.

ARSEI. All right…

He takes a few steps and bumps into SAMSON's *legs. He falls down and jumps up again in fear.*

What the fuck…? Mortko, there's something alive over here.

He jumps back to a safe distance and looks with horror at the window and the two legs hanging out of it.

MORTKO. And you said nightingales.

He goes over to the legs and taps on them. The legs react.

Alive. Aha! So who does this fine strong set of pins belong to?

ARSEI. Samson, is that you?

There is a bellowing in answer.

(*With relief.*) Samson. Thank God for that... And what's the scoundrel up to?

MORTKO (*calmly*). Stealing the grain, that's what. He got stuck.

YUKHIM, *one of the guards who has come round somewhat, starts roaring indistinctly and pointing at* SAMSON*'s legs.*

YUKHIM. He got me drunk... The bastard... Not my fault...

ARSEI *begins laughing.* MORTKO *laughs with him.* MORTKO *stops laughing first.*

MORTKO. What are you laughing at? The man's in pain. He needs pulling out. Or, you know what? Put a match between his toes and singe him a bit. He'll come shooting out like a bullet.

ARSEI *laughs.*

ARSEI. He's my godfather. It wouldn't be kind.

MORTKO (*frowning*). What kind of Soviet activist has a godfather?

ARSEI (*confused*). Well, he's... almost a relative.

MORTKO. A relative, is he? Well, you can pull him out, then. I'm not going to kill myself.

ARSEI *grabs* SAMSON*'s legs and pulls him out with a bit of effort.*

In the background, YUKHIM *is trying to wake* GAVRILO. *He is unsuccessful.* GAVRILO *is in a deep sleep.*

YUKHIM. Gavrilo... Gavrilo... Get up... We're in the fucking shit...

ARSEI and MORTKO *help* SAMSON *out.* SAMSON, *redfaced and dirty, sits on the ground and breathes heavily.*

ARSEI. How could you, Samson, do something like this?

MORTKO. Your mate Gorobets took to his heels, did he?

SAMSON. I was on my own...

MORTKO. Well, well... On your own. Then you can answer for both of you. Hey, Yukhim – have you sobered up yet?

YUKHIM. I'm as fresh as a daisy, me...

He gets up with great difficulty and stands there, swaying.

MORTKO. So, Samson got you drunk?

YUKHIM. Bastard got me drunk. Forced it down my throat. Knew my weakness.

SAMSON. What you fucking around for? I never forced you to drink. You saw the bottle and sucked it all up like a snake.

MORTKO. And I've been looking at you all this while, Samson, and wondering to myself. Where do you get your good health? And now I know. You were stealing it from the State.

SAMSON. If the State needs this grain, then why is it rotting in here? It's rotten. Perhaps you didn't know that?

MORTKO. That's got nothing to do with you. If that's how it is, then that's how it's supposed to be.

SAMSON. But people are dying like flies.

MORTKO. Those aren't people. They're enemies, like you.

SAMSON. What sort of enemy am I? I'm like everyone else. I want to eat.

MORTKO. You're an individualist. Thinking about your belly.

ARSEI. He won't do it again, will you, Samson?

SAMSON. I won't.

MORTKO. You won't do it again? Well, that's a good boy, then. Where are you off to? Stop. Yukhim, you know you could be shot for falling asleep at your post?

YUKHIM. I won't do it again either, Mortko… I bloody won't…

MORTKO. You're like little children. 'I won't do it again.' What a good boy. I hope at least you didn't swap your rifle for a bottle?

YUKHIM. Here it is.

MORTKO. Is it loaded?

YUKHIM. Course!

MORTKO. What a hero. Right, turn to face the wall, Samson. Or, no, if you want you can stand like that. In the name of the Soviet, I sentence you to death by shooting. Yukhim, carry out the sentence.

They all look at MORTKO *in amazement.*

YUKHIM. What?

MORTKO. Just do it, man. No questions.

ARSEI. That's enough, Mortko.

MORTKO. Don't you get it?

ARSEI. Well… I… you…

MORTKO *turns around slowly and looks at* ARSEI.

MORTKO. Arsei, I just don't understand you… A State criminal was caught right in front of you and you're standing here mumbling like a goat.

ARSEI. But there's… there's a court.

MORTKO. Surely you know that I represent the Soviet in this village and I have the power to sentence and carry out the sentence without any court proceedings.

ARSEI. But it's rotten. What's the point in killing someone for some rotten grain?

MORTKO. You have no consciousness, Comrade Pechoritsa. You worry me. We need to have a serious conversation. Later. Yukhim, what have you stopped for?

YUKHIM. I... Well, I can't...

MORTKO. Not your godfather, too?

YUKHIM. He's my neighbour...

MORTKO. Ah! A good neighbour. 'Love thy neighbour', eh? You tell me, Yukhim, when you'd drunk yourself to destitution and your wife had gone begging round the village, who pulled you out of the gutter? Gave you work when there was practically nothing left of you? Your neighbour?

YUKHIM. You, Mortko.

MORTKO. Wrong answer. The Soviet State took pity on you, saved you from death. And you sleep on duty and help criminals.

YUKHIM. I'll do it!

He lifts the gun and aims. Then he lowers it.

Could he turn his back to us?

MORTKO (*to* SAMSON). Turn round!

SAMSON. Why?

ARSEI. Mortko, give it up, eh? They're all scared shitless by now.

MORTKO. Are you going to keep us hanging around, Yukhim?

ARSEI. It was a joke, lads!

YUKHIM *takes aim with shaking hands, and shoots at* SAMSON, *who is bent double with fear. The bullet passes him closely. The nightingales are silent. It is suddenly noticeable that dawn is coming.*

MORTKO. Oh. It's getting light.

>YUKHIM *looks at his gun with horror.* SAMSON *looks at* YUKHIM. ARSEI *looks at the smiling* MORTKO.

>Well, you're a useless bloody guard. Take the thief off to the lock-up. We'll work out what to do with him tomorrow. Are your ears working? No, stop a minute. What shall we do with Gavrilo?

ARSEI. Let him sleep.

MORTKO. Good. 'Let him sleep.' Come on, then, lads, let's have him in the grain store instead of Samson.

>YUKHIM *and* SAMSON *giggle nervously, exchanging glances.*

>What's wrong with you, boys, I don't know... no sense of humour, eh? Push him in head-first. He's skinny, he'll fit through.

>YUKHIM *and* SAMSON *take the drunken, sleeping* GAVRILO *and stuff him through the opening. There is the sound of his body falling onto something soft.*

>*The four of them laugh for a long time.*

>Right, then, we've had our fun. Yukhim, you take our thief off to the lock-up and we'll work out later what to do with him.

SAMSON. Let me go, sir! I'd be better off going home. You won't see me here again, on my word, I guarantee it!

MORTKO. I don't believe your words or your guarantees. You can go and sit in our lock-up and contemplate your life, rather than your belly. Lead him away, Yukhim.

>YUKHIM *obediently pushes the obedient* SAMSON *in front of him.* MORTKO *watches them leave with contempt.*

>Watch that. Off he goes like a sheep. He could run off into the forest. I would.

ARSEI. Mortko, how could you? He could have shot him.

>*He moves away from* MORTKO *in his confusion.*

MORTKO. Spare the rod. Got to teach them. I knew he would miss. He's cack-handed, and anyway he was aiming at me more than anyone. But I wasn't shaking like you are now. What's wrong with you, why are you giving me that wolf-look? It's easy to stay out of it all. It's easy to *seem* kind. Can't you see I'm doing work here that no one else will do, but without it the next step is impossible? Maybe no one will remember me afterwards with a kind word. Afterwards, when we've arrived, achieved our goal. They'll remember the others – you, and even Gavrilo, but they won't remember me. Or they'll curse my memory if they do. And no one will appreciate the sacrifice I made for the future of this wretched country of mine...

ARSEI. I understand it all with my mind, Mortko. But when it's in my own village... it's difficult, can't you see? I'd like to go somewhere else... somewhere where I don't know anyone and they don't know me...

MORTKO. You want it easy, you want a clear conscience. And you need to earn that. But for now... Look and learn.

MORTKO *lifts the boards ripped from the window and fixes them back over the window.* ARSEI *looks. He learns.*

It grows dark. There is just the sound of some muffled blows from above, a rustling and a groan.

GAVRILO. Shit. Where am I?

He screams out in panic. There is the sound of him scattering the mice.

Fucking hell... Get out of it! Shoo! Shoo! Fuck... Where am I, for the love of God?

His eyes gradually become used to the darkness. There is a weak light trickling through the poorly boarded upper windows.

GAVRILO *is sitting on a large pile of grain. There is grain everywhere. A lot of grain.*

Angels are looking down pityingly from the ceiling.

GAVRILO, *in a drunken stupor, looks in horror from side to side. He gropes at the ground around him and tries to make out what has happened.*

(*In a trembling voice.*) What was it happened…? First that bastard Gorobets came over and asked us for a few grains of corn. Yukhim told him to fuck off. Then Samson came along and left a bottle of moonshine. We agreed on tomorrow. That tomorrow they'd be along for the grain. We had a drink and they went. And then we had some more. We were having a chat. Talking about women. Yukhim was moaning about his wife. She was having an affair with a kulak, that Onis'ko Staritskii. He's no longer alive. But she lost her mind with the hunger. So Yukhim joined the activists and started bringing home twenty-five per cent and once his wife had filled her belly she went round sleeping with everyone. Filthy bitch she is. He rescued her from death and that was her thank you. He beat her hard. Now she's much better behaved. And we drank some more and had some pig fat and remembered how Mortko shot the kulaks. Staritskii Feodosii, Onis'ko, Mel'nik Kilina… She was a pretty girl. I wanted to marry her, but the silly fool wouldn't join the collective… Her dad had a couple of cows, a horse and a bit of land, and they didn't want to lose the cows. They died for the cows. Then we drank a bit more. Mortko promised that if we work for a year then he'll send us to town for promotion. So we were dreaming about how good our life would be compared to the rest of them. Everyone in our village is a miserable wretch… Hah! And then we drank some more and decided we'd go and get old Teklia the hunchback. Yukhim is always after loving when he's had too much. And what happened then? I've forgotten. Anything could have happened. Perhaps there was a storm and I was hit by lightning. Someone could have come to get some grain and murdered me. One thing is sure: I must have been killed in my sleep. And I'm in heaven. No, in hell. It'd be lighter in heaven. And it's dark here. So I suppose now I'm going to have to answer for my sins.

Perhaps it is the mice, or perhaps GAVRILO's *movements, but suddenly at that moment the mountain of grain starts slipping down from one of the walls and slowly reveals a wall-painted iconostasis. Light from the wall pours onto* GAVRILO *and in this light the faces of the Mother of God and her baby appear – right opposite* GAVRILO *and at about his height.* GAVRILO *is frozen in a drunken religious ecstasy.*

Who is it? Lord God... Mother of God... Have you come down to me?

GAVRILO *falls down, unconscious.*

End of Act One.

ACT TWO

16 April 1933

A graveyard on a hill. There are many freshly dug graves. On some there are crosses, but on the whole they have no markings – little mounds of earth show the location of the graves. It is beautiful there. The cherry blossom is out. The birds are singing.

MOKRINA and ARSEI are sitting by one of the graves and kissing. There is no cross on this grave, just the earth. There are many like this. And more and more larger mass graves. There is one completely new grave which is still empty.

ARTYUKH the gravedigger drives his cart over to this grave and throws a few corpses from his cart into the grave.

MOKRINA pulls away from the kiss and gives a tired and happy sigh.

MOKRINA. What have you brought?

> *ARSEI unties the bundle and sets it out. It contains bread, pig fat, onion. ARSEI chops it very thinly. MOKRINA wants to take some but ARSEI gently pushes her away and feeds her from his own hands.*

ARSEI. I'll do it. Or you'll eat too much and be ill again.

MOKRINA. Thank you... thank you, if it wasn't for you...
How I love you, Arsei...

ARSEI. My own sweet cherry.

> *He kisses her chewing mouth. MOKRINA laughs and presses against him fondly.*

> *ARTYUKH throws the last body into the hole with great difficulty. He loses his balance and falls in together with the body. His weak cries can be heard.*

I told you we'd be together. We'll have a proper life. We'll
live well.

MOKRINA *eats. As she eats, her expression becomes
increasingly set and bitter. ARSEI doesn't see this – he is
looking dreamily at the village from the hill.*

(*Dreamily.*) When the famine is over, we'll go and live in
town. Mortko promised that the activists will study for free.
And we'll get a place to live. Rations. We'll live together.
We'll take Mother. Mine and yours. Everything will be
different, d'you realise? Everyone will get the same. No
envying other people. I'm saving, I am. Saving up for our
life together, our happy future...

MOKRINA *stops chewing, as if she was choking. There is a
look of horror on her face. She throws herself on the grave
and sobs.*

MOKRINA. Father! Forgive me! Sitting here with your
murderer! Eating bread and fat! And you, worn to death,
Father! When will you take me with you?!

ARSEI (*hurt*). Mokrina, when you're hungry, you're the
sweetest, kindest love, but as soon as your belly's full you
turn into a witch. Perhaps I'd be better off keeping you
hungry, eh? I never killed your father. Besides, what would
have happened to you, if it hadn't been for me!?

MOKRINA *throws the rest of the food at him.*

MOKRINA. Bastard! I don't want any of it! Hate you!

ARSEI (*wearily*). Not that old song. Come on, pick it up – take
it back to your mother. You've eaten too much, you're
getting upset. What am I going to do with you? And I had a
lollipop for you.

MOKRINA. I don't want it! Don't want anything!

ARSEI *takes a lollipop out of his jacket pocket and teases
MOKRINA with it. MOKRINA reaches out for it.*

ARSEI. Kiss me, and it's yours.

MOKRINA *kisses* ARSEI *quickly and takes the lollipop.*
ARSEI *helps her collect up the spilt food into a cloth.*

Go home. Don't go through the woods. They're full of
murderers. Come back here the day after tomorrow. I'll bring
something.

MOKRINA. Oh! There's some men coming…

ARSEI. Quick, Mokrina – it's our lot coming. Mortko must
have called for me. I don't want them to see us together…

MOKRINA. Curse your Mortko.

MOKRINA *stands and, staggering, leaves.* YUKHIM *and*
RUDENKO *appear on horses.*

RUDENKO. There you are! With your little girl, eh? Mortko
sent for you.

ARSEI. That urgent?

RUDENKO (*excitedly*). It is, it is. News from the District – and
they heard from the Region, and they heard from Moscow…
That's how big it is… An American journalist is coming
here.

ARSEI. Where, here? To our village? From America? Have
they gone completely mad?

RUDENKO. Well, that's nothing to do with us. This journalist,
he writes for the whole American nation all about Soviet
achievements. He's even interviewed Stalin himself. He's
coming here so he can see with his own eyes… that…
(*Himself amazed.*) there's no famine…

ARSEI. Have you been drinking? Do you know what you're
saying? What about these people lying in pits, then? Are they
drunk?

YUKHIM. Well… That's what's come down to us from above.
And we mustn't let the side down.

ARSEI. Maybe he'll go somewhere else?

YUKHIM. It's the same everywhere, isn't it?

ARSEI. I don't know what to say. It's like a bad joke.

RUDENKO. Anyway, Arsei, Mortko has decided me and you are responsible for this. He said that if we do a good job, he'll send us to town straightaway. Out of this hell... The American is coming in a week's time.

ARSEI *spits angrily.*

ARSEI. Maybe he should come in a year's time. We'll all be living in paradise by then.

RUDENKO. No corpses anywhere. No starving people. We want a Soviet village with a club, dancing, a canteen. Progressive youth. They'll send us everything we need. Food and clothes and all. We need to find the agit-brigade and bring them here. Where are they now, have you heard?

ARSEI. I have. Stuck in Bairak. Their horses were stolen and eaten. So they're stuck.

ARTYUKH *climbs out of the pit. Clearly he must have piled the bodies one on top of the other so he could climb out. He gets on his cart. An exhausted, stringy-looking nag pulls it slowly away from the graveyard.*

RUDENKO. Good. We'll have to send for them, then. Yukhim, you can go. And find them some horses.

YUKHIM. Where will I find horses?

RUDENKO. You'll have to collectivise someone. Take Artyukh's. It's not as close to death as it looks.

YUKHIM. What? How's Artyukh going to do his job?

RUDENKO. All right. It was only a joke. Mortko will get you a car. And we'll put together such a show that that American won't want to leave.

ARSEI. Don't be ridiculous.

YUKHIM. What will we tell people?

RUDENKO. Mortko will think of something. He said we didn't have to worry about that.

ARSEI. I just don't understand, though. Why's he coming here? Why's this curse fallen on us?

RUDENKO (*genuinely surprised*). Why? Just look around you! Is there a better village anywhere?! Just look at our beautiful river! What a river it is, eh?! Winding through the meadows like a snake. And such picturesque banks! If I was an artist I'd be painting it all… And the fish in our river! Like this, they are, and I'm not lying… Sometimes you go down to the flats at dawn and the beauty of it almost knocks you for six… The pale mist blankets the ground, covering the sleeping swans in its softness. And our forest, it's like a fortress wall. With a forest like that you'd not be scared of anything! I mean, honestly. Sometimes I look down at our village from this hill and I forget everything in my happiness. If there is a better village anywhere in the world, well, it certainly isn't in the Ukraine! And definitely not in America. And the people are good people. And the land is fertile… Poke a stick in the ground and it'd burst into flower.

He digs a stick into FEODOSII's *grave, in place of a cross.* ARSEI *and* YUKHIM *look at it stupidly as if they were waiting for it to burst into bud.*

Three springs from now there'll be sparrows nesting in that. And lovers sitting under it.

ARSEI *and* YUKHIM *stare at* RUDENKO *in amazement.*

GAVRILO *comes walking past the graves. He looks unkempt, odd, wild.*

He has a light in his eyes. He is muttering. Talking to someone.

(*Cheerfully.*) There's your mate, Yukhim. Hey, Gavrilo, how was the grain store? Who let you out?

GAVRILO. She did. She let me out.

ARSEI. Stop, Rudenko. Something's wrong with him...

RUDENKO. Has he gone mad? What you muttering there?

GAVRILO. I'm praying.

RUDENKO. Gavrilo is praying. Well, there's one for the books. What you praying for? A glass of vodka?

GAVRILO. Not for myself...

RUDENKO. I see. Pray out loud so we can hear.

GAVRILO. All right.

> GAVRILO *turns and speaks to an invisible person before him. He speaks simply and as if to a friend.*

> Lord, forgive me and have pity on me. Forgive me, whore that I am, that I went with a kulak... My husband is a miserable drunkard, he doesn't work, he just sits and drinks. But Onis'ko Staritskii – he's a good man, hard-working, he's got hands of gold, when he puts them round me my heart stops. I'd have gone to the end of the world for him if they hadn't killed him... I'm a fallen woman, I am, a stupid woman; forgive me and have pity on me, Lord. I didn't know it was such a sin to betray a bad husband. Now my husband hates those kulaks and they pay him good money for his hate... I stopped going out of the house after he beat me the last time. Who wants me now with my broken nose?

RUDENKO. He's lost his mind. Praying like a woman.

YUKHIM (*pale and frightened*). That's my wife praying. He's speaking for her. I can hear her voice.

RUDENKO. I think we'll have to find a place to hide our comrade when this American turns up.

ARSEI. Back in the grain store?

> ARSEI *and* RUDENKO *laugh.* YUKHIM *doesn't.*

23 April 1933

The square in front of the village Soviet and the reading room. A radio speaker is playing cheerful music to the square. The reading room has a new sign which reads: 'CANTEEN'. The Soviet, reading room and church grain store are all decorated in red flags. The houses have been freshly painted. The square has become smart and Soviet. PEOPLE, *or what remains of people, are drawn to the square from all sides. Some of them walk themselves, some are led, others chased in by the* ACTIVISTS.

A tribune stands on the square and behind it stands MORTKO. YUKHIM *stands in front of the tribune. A group of strong, healthy* ACTIVISTS *stand behind and to one side is the agit-brigade's truck.* MORTKO *surveys the* CROWD *critically.*

MORTKO (*to* RUDENKO). I said to come dressed in their best. Look at them!

RUDENKO. I told them but they laughed.

MORTKO. I've gathered you here today, comrades, for a very serious reason. Our Government has decided to bestow a great honour on this village. Our little village has been chosen from thousands of others to be the site of a new film about the future happy life of the Soviet peasantry. So what does this mean for us? It means that we have the opportunity to show ourselves in the best light possible. It also means that we have some duties to do. Firstly, I asked you all to put on your Sunday best. Ladies! Where are your frocks and white blouses? Where are your necklaces? Surely you haven't fallen this far?

VOICES. We haven't got any.

Nothing left.

Are you making fun of us?

We swapped it all for food.

MORTKO. Right. We'll give you clothes. *Lend* them to you. Anyone who really excels themselves might get to keep something as a souvenir.

VOICE. What do we have to do?

MORTKO. Nothing too difficult. Walk about, sing, dance… like our actors. You've seen our actors performing, haven't you?

GOROBETS. How about food?

MORTKO. There'll be food. And tea to drink. And wine. Look – they're laying the tables already. Meat, herrings, potatoes, pies.

The CROWD *groans.*

But of course, if anyone feels too weak, or unsure of themselves, they can go home. This is all strictly voluntary and by your consent. The new regime would not dream of forcing anyone. You are free to refuse and go home.

Nobody moves.

Our comrades the agitators will help you achieve the correct appearance: they'll make you up and give you your roles and tasks. The cameramen will be here later on, but for now you can prepare yourselves and rehearse a little.

OLIANA. What's going on…? They're talking so strangely… Maybe I've lost my mind like poor old Gavrilo…

SAMOILENKO. Is the food at the rehearsal going to be real food?

GOROBETS. It won't be human flesh, so you can go home.

SAMOILENKO (*squealing*). Prove it, prove it first!

The CROWD *had distanced themselves from* SAMOILENKO *from the start but now they move even further away from her.*

MORTKO. No, there won't be any food at the rehearsal, only during the filming. We can't allow ourselves endless feasting in these difficult times. And another thing... not all of you will be suitable for this film. Some of you don't suit at all. But don't upset yourselves about this. Not everyone has the talent.

GOROBETS. We're all talented, Comrade Mortko. We're a very talented nation.

OLIANA. How am I going to dance? I was carried here in someone's arms.

MASHA steps out of the truck. She is heavily pregnant.

MASHA. Comrades, make an orderly queue. These clothes are on loan only, do you hear me? On loan! These costumes must be returned straight after the filming.

She chooses the youngest and those still standing on their own two feet. Amongst them is MOKRINA.

You, girl. And you. And you. In a queue, please. Right. Come in when I call you.

* * *

The tent. A makeshift dressing room. In one corner is a pile of worn, but clean, clothing. Three GIRLS sit in the middle on benches. One of them is MOKRINA.

MASHA traces brows on them and goes round their eyes with black coal. She rubs their cheeks with beetroot and carrot. She stuffs rags down their flat fronts.

YURKO is watching cheerfully and without embarrassment, helping MASHA choose clothes for the GIRLS.

YURKO. Mokrina's got enough tit on her already. There – take the prettiest blouse and skirt.

He gets them out of the pile, choosing the prettiest things for MOKRINA. The other GIRLS purse their lips in annoyance.

MASHA. Not one hole or stain on these. You must give them back. These are from the district club's clothes for actors.

GIRL 1. Let me…

She takes the carrot from MASHA *and scrubs her cheeks with it.*

GIRL 2 (*quietly*). Let me have those boots.

YURKO. They're men's boots.

GIRL 2. Doesn't matter, give them here.

YURKO throws the boots to her. GIRL 2 *looks at them carefully.*

(*To* MOKRINA.) These are my granddad's boots. He was wearing them when the Communists took him away. Look – it even says here: 'G. Prut'ko'.

MOKRINA. Keep quiet. Or you'll stay hungry.

GIRL 2 (*loudly*). These are my granddad's boots! Grigoriia Prut'ko. It says so here!

IVAN IVANYCH (*entering*). Who's making all the fuss in here? Who's spoiling things? Right, love, off you go. You're not going to be in the show.

GIRL 2. What? I only said these were my granddad's boots. They killed him in these and then they took them off him. What's wrong with saying that?

IVAN IVANYCH *and* VASILII *take the rouged-up* GIRL 2 *under the arms, take away the boots and lead her out of the tent.* GIRL 2 *resists as much as she can.*

Give me the boots back at least! Give them back! What did I say?

During this incident there is a distinct crunching sound. MASHA *turns round and sees* GIRL 1 *eating the 'make-up' – the carrot and beetroot.*

MASHA. Oh, you little idiot! Stupid little idiot! And you could have been eating meat! Where am I going to get my make-up from? Get out of here! And don't come back without make-up.

GIRL 1 *is also led out.* MOKRINA *is left on her own.*

VASILII. There's a good girl. Nice, clever, quiet girl.

YURKO. And beautiful.

IVAN IVANYCH. I remember you. Remember when we came. And you sang to us beautifully. You can sing today. But something cheery. Is that agreed?

MOKRINA. If I don't eat I can't sing.

IVAN IVANYCH. We'll feed you. So how's it going with your God, then?

MOKRINA. Not good.

IVAN IVANYCH. So is there a God or not? What do you think now?

MOKRINA. There's no God. You were all right. If there was a God, d'you think you'd be making this film?

IVAN IVANYCH. There, see. I told you so, didn't I?

An OLD WOMAN *comes into the tent. She can hardly stand.*

MASHA. What you here for, old girl?

OLD WOMAN. What do you mean? I'm an actress.

MASHA. Are we making a comedy? What do you think you're up to? Go on, back home. Your grandsons are waiting for you.

OLD WOMAN. What are you whispering about?

IVAN IVANYCH (*loudly*). I'm afraid you aren't suitable. Goodbye.

OLD WOMAN. What do you mean, not 'suitable'? Why ever not? I can sing, I can dance.

IVAN IVANYCH. Old lady, you can hardly stand up. Don't make us laugh. We need young people and cheerful songs.

OLD WOMAN. I'm still young. And I can sing such cheerful songs that you'll wet yourself with laughing.

The OLD WOMAN *stops in the middle of the room and breaks into song.*

(*Singing.*)
> Where two poplars in a meadow,
> Stood and two boys lay, so,
> Spent their time in idle talk,
> And dares and drinking, heigh-ho!
>
> A cuckoo on a branch up high,
> Did hit them where they lay, so,
> Sticks and stones they threw up high,
> And down came bird shit, heigh-ho!
>
> Lida, Lida, on a horse,
> And behind her boys did play, so,
> She tickled them with a riding crop,
> About their faces, heigh-ho!
>
> Here's Tamara, she went far,
> Till the boys did want their way, so,
> She took them by the – hey Tamara –
> Took them by the – heigh-ho!

Everyone is stunned by her singing. The OLD WOMAN *even begins to dance. On the last note, the most difficult and peculiar dance step, the* OLD WOMAN *drops down dead.*

IVAN IVANYCH (*to* VASILII). What a to-do. Get that body out of here. No bloody peace and quiet to work in.

VASILII *drags out the* OLD WOMAN*'s body.*

MOKRINA (*quietly, to* YURKO). Can I give those boots to my friend?

YURKO *wraps the boots in a rag and hands them to her, unnoticed.*

* * *

*The square in front of the village Soviet. The square and the
buildings are decorated with red flags. Signs saying 'CLUB'
and 'SHOP' have been added to the one saying 'CANTEEN'. A
covered area by the 'canteen' has been set up and long tables
have been covered with white cloths. Long benches run
alongside the tables. There are plates on the tables. Smoke
rises from the canteen's chimney, the stove is firing, the
celebration is being prepared. MASHA, YURKO and VASILII
are carrying out plates of steaming food and placing them on
the table.*

*MORTKO is standing on the tribune. A row of well-dressed
PEOPLE are standing in front of him. Their hollow cheeks are
painted and the MEN are clean-shaven with neat hair. They
look distractedly at MORTKO, who is examining them
sceptically.*

RUDENKO (*uncertainly*). Perhaps we should give them all a
    spoon of porridge.

MORTKO (*reproachfully*). Comrade Rudenko, surely you know
    what will happen if we do that. They'll eat their spoon and
    fall asleep right in the square. How did the rehearsal go?

IVAN IVANYCH (*sighing*). They've all gone stupid. They used
    to be much quicker.

MORTKO. You're the stupid one. Are you saying, then, that the
    kulaks were clever and the poor are stupid?

IVAN IVANYCH. Let me be struck down on the spot if that's
    what I thought. That girl over there is very sharp. She's
    going to sing and the rest are going to take up the song. The
    dancing isn't quite there. But everyone is able to move, at
    least.

RUDENKO. We're worried about the food, too. They'll throw
    themselves on it, you won't get them off it if you drag them
    by the ears. That American will think they're starving.
    They'll spoil the whole effect. Maybe we should feed them
    first?

MORTKO. Do you think I'm a monster? If there was something to feed them with I would, but we've only got enough for one portion each. So they can wait patiently.

They can live in hope. You've collected up enough bloody cripples, haven't you…? Wasn't there anyone who looked even remotely well-fed? It's just upsetting, what that American is going to think of us. He's going to write what a pathetic nation we are, us Ukrainians…

RUDENKO. Let Samson out of jail. He's still got a good sizeable girth on him.

MORTKO. Good thinking. Yukhim, bring Samson here. Tell him, if he can play the part of a Soviet strongman, then I'll forgive him.

YUKHIM *runs off joyfully towards the prison.*

(*Turning to the* CROWD.) Dear comrades. Look at the faces on you. Could you crack a smile? We need your smiles.

Everyone smiles with their mouth only.

And now, let's see what Ivan Ivanych has been teaching you.

IVAN IVANYCH (*into a loudspeaker*). Right. Everyone take their places. Gather your strength for a last run-through.

VOICES. There's no strength left to gather.

Stop making fun of all of us!

Give us some meat!

IVAN IVANYCH. Hecklers and spoilers will not be allowed to take part. Take your places, everyone.

They take their places. Someone picks up a yoke, OLIANA *comes out of the Soviet holding a postbag,* MEN WITH SPADES *return home from a day's work at the collective farm,* LARGE-BREASTED WOMEN *come home with buckets from the farm, amongst them* MOKRINA. *It is a caricature of the life which will be lived out here a few decades later.*

Mokrina, sing.

MOKRINA (*singing*).
> We were born to make a fairy tale come true,
> We were born to master space and sky,
> We were winged in steel by our reason,
> With the surging of a motor where our heart should beat
>> inside.

> Up, up and ever on,
> Soaring like birds from the ground,
> And in each propeller the deepest breath,
> Of the country sleeping sound.

The CROWD *pick up the song and start singing.*
GOROBETS *plays on the accordion.*

A few CRIPPLES *come to the front of the* CROWD *and dance pathetically to the music.*

IVAN IVANYCH (*into his loudspeaker*). Right, now over to the table, everyone, at a nice even pace.

The CROWD *rush for the table in a chaotic tumult of bodies.*

No running! I said, no running! Stop! Back to your places. Right, until you learn to carry out my commands, no one is sitting down at the table.

Everyone returns to their places and starts again.

MASHA. Mokrina, from the beginning.

MOKRINA (*singing*).
> We were born to make a fairy tale come true,
> We were born to master space and sky,
> We were winged in steel by our reason,
> With the surging of a motor where our heart should beat
>> inside.

> Up, up and ever on,
> Soaring like birds from the ground,
> And in each propeller the deepest breath,
> Of the country sleeping sound.

The others take up the song. The DANCERS *put their last strength into dancing.*

IVAN IVANYCH (*into his loudspeaker*). Right – now to the table. Slowly.

The CROWD *moves unnaturally slowly towards the table, where plates of potatoes and fried meat and lots of other forgotten delicacies are steaming.*

MORTKO. No, stop! I don't like your dancers. Is that the dance of the dying kulak or something? Where's your passion? Your dedication? You're a disgrace, you're going to let us down in front of the whole of America!

RUDENKO. Podgornii, Soroka, what's wrong with you – are you both going soft? You're the best dancers in the area. You used to perform – you danced for our comrades in the district.

PODGORNII. That's when we were eating two meals a day.

MORTKO. Can you think about nothing else?

EVERYONE. No.

MOKRINA starts singing again.

The others take up the refrain.

The DANCERS *dance.*

At IVAN IVANYCH's *command, they all walk slowly towards the table. Some remain lying on the ground.*

MORTKO. I did warn you! Not everyone was suitable for this. But no, you all had to beat each other to it. If you don't have the strength you can leave us now. (*To his* ASSISTANTS.) Clear the square of non-participants.

They carry off the bodies.

RUDENKO. Listen, Mortko, if they have to dance any more we'll be left without dancers altogether.

MORTKO. You'll be dancing, then.

IVAN IVANYCH (*into his loudspeaker*). Carry on moving towards the table. Let's have some talking amongst yourselves. You in the red trousers, embrace that woman over there.

MAN. She's not mine.

IVAN IVANYCH. I'm not asking you to marry her. I said put your arm round her.

The MAN *embraces the* WOMAN.

OLIANA. Can someone put their arm round me too, or I'll fall over.

The weakest WOMEN *are supported by the* MEN *and vice versa. The impression of an extremely loving community is created.*

MORTKO (*pleased*). That's the ticket!

IVAN IVANYCH. Now let's hear something Ukrainian. Folksy. Foreigners love all that traditional stuff.

OLIANA (*singing*).
The Cossacks came riding past, back from the River Don,
And took Galia with them, lured by their song.

Oh, sweet Galia, still a young girl!
Took Galia with them, lured by their song.

She chokes and is silent. She starts again. She tries very hard, but it doesn't sound good.

MORTKO *frowns.* IVAN IVANYCH *shrugs guiltily.*

Just at this moment, YUKHIM *leads* SAMSON *onto the square.* SAMSON *has lost a lot of weight, but he still seems big and strong compared to the rest of them. There is an expression of joy and surprise on his face.* GOROBETS *rushes happily towards him.*

GOROBETS. Samson! You're half the size you were!

SAMSON. Would I fit through that window now?

They laugh.

MASHA (*with love*). Here's my Samson. And I thought he was being eaten by worms. Hey, Samson, I've got news for you.

She pats her belly.

Remember we spent the night together in the club last autumn?

SAMSON. Leave me alone, woman – who haven't you spent the night with?!

MASHA. Fool. This is yours.

SAMSON. I lived fifteen years with my old lady and she never gave me anything, and I only went with you once.

MASHA. Oh, I couldn't care less, you bleating on like that. A Soviet woman doesn't need a husband. I've got all my comrades to look after me.

She shakes her hand dismissively at him and gets into the truck. SAMSON *looks around the square and sees the well-dressed people locked in embraces, the tables under an awning.*

SAMSON. What's going on, tell me... Gorobets, did the famine end whilst I was in jail?

OLIANA (*laughing*). That's it! In one moment the whole thing was over.

Everyone laughs at SAMSON's *naivety.*

SAMSON. Are these tables laid for us?

MORTKO. For you...

SAMSON. I've forgotten when I last ate.

MORTKO. You'll remember. Only, first you have to take part in our celebration. Sing, Samson. A new life has begun!

SAMSON. Well, in that case I won't just sing, I'll dance, too!

SAMSON in his joy sings out in his strong voice. Those who can, take up the tune.

(Singing.)

The Cossacks came riding past, back from the River Don,
And took Galia with them, lured by their song.

Oh, sweet Galia, still a young girl!
Took Galia with them, lured by their song.

Come with us, Galia, and we'll go together,
And it'll be better than with your own mother!

Oh, sweet Galia, still a young girl!
It'll be better than with your own mother!

They carried Galia to the forest glades,
And they tied Galia to a tree by her braids.

Oh, sweet Galia, still a young girl!
And they tied Galia to a tree by her braids.

There they set to work to gather dry shoots,
And they set light to that tree from its crown to its roots.

Oh, sweet Galia, still a young girl!
They set light to that tree from its crown to its roots.

MORTKO is in seventh heaven.

MORTKO (*reproaching* IVAN IVANYCH). There! You see!
Can't even put on a show without Mortko.

He takes the loudspeaker from IVAN IVANYCH.

(*Into the loudspeaker.*) Move! That's it! Move! You lot in
front of the Soviet, you turn right; and you lot by the old
church, you turn left to meet them, and we'll have a nice
pattern.

*The CROWD is more cheerful now, and the whole thing
comes to life.*

GOROBETS (*to* SAMSON). Thank you, Samson, me boy, you've helped us all out, things'll go faster now. Only this morning, you won't believe it, they were chasing us round and they wouldn't even give us bread. Felt like climbing into Artyukh's cart myself.

At this moment a car drives into the square. It contains ARSEI *and the* DRIVER.

MORTKO (*agitated*). Why is it just Arsei? Where's the American? Where's the local representative? Where's all the rest?

RUDENKO. Maybe they're in another car behind?

IVAN IVANYCH (*into his loudspeaker*). Don't stop, comrades, the cameramen will be here soon. Get back to your places.

The action continues. A YOUNG MAN *acts as* MOKRINA's *lover and they dance together.*

ARSEI, *highly agitated, jumps out of the car and runs to* MORTKO.

MORTKO. Well? Where are they all? You didn't miss the train, did you?

ARSEI (*catching his breath*). I got there an hour early... I waited and the train came in, but only a few women got out... I went to the area Soviet and they started ringing Poltava, and it turned out that the trip was cancelled, and they didn't have time to tell us. They told me to stop everything and not to wait. Seems like no one is coming.

MORTKO. 'Not to wait'? What do they think...? Blast. What the hell is going on?! And what am I going to do with all this theatre now? Ivan Ivanych!

IVAN IVANYCH. Well then. Let's dismiss them all. Only, what are we going to do with all the tables? The food?

ARSEI. They asked me to tell you that Comrade Petrenko from the Regional Soviet would be here with some other comrades, so they need to be properly welcomed...

MORTKO (*after consideration*). So our efforts weren't wasted, then. Right. (*To* IVAN IVANYCH.) Go and quietly give orders in the kitchen for everything to be taken back. Lock it all up and get it guarded. Arsei, Yukhim, stand by the doors and don't let anyone in. And I'll make a speech.

IVAN IVANYCH goes into the canteen. ARSEI and YUKHIM, exchanging glances, silent and without much enthusiasm, follow IVAN IVANYCH.

Dear comrades!

The CROWD is either so caught up with the artistry of the presentation or so mortally exhausted that they don't register straightaway that they are being addressed and should stop.

Wonderful. Well, how could we improve on that?!

You've put a hundred-per-cent effort into the task and when I file my report to the Region I'm going to write that the inhabitants of this village had the artistic approach and the enthusiasm of true Soviet citizens. With clear consciences and the sense of a job well done, you may all now have a rest.

SAMSON. What a day! What a day! Hurray for the Soviet Government!

But apart from SAMSON, no one else expresses particular joy.

GOROBETS. You hang on with your shouting. (*To* MORTKO.) Rest? Where? When's the filming going to start?

MORTKO. The filming is not happening today. Filming will be tomorrow. So you've been lucky indeed today, and you're getting off early. Tomorrow, now…

OLIANA (*wailing*). Good people! They're hiding the food away in the hall!

The CROWD turn their heads in the direction of the tables. An indignant murmuring begins.

MORTKO. What's so hard to understand? Make your way, please. Nothing's going to vanish before tomorrow. We'll have a real feast tomorrow! But please hand back all your clothes to Masha. And let's be quick about it. Please don't make me angry, comrades.

A few WOMEN *obediently leave the* CROWD *and move towards the truck.* MASHA *goes over to* GIRL 1, *who takes off her scarf and gives it to* MASHA. *She goes to the second* GIRL 2 *and waits while she takes off her boots and gives them back. Then a few more. Finally she gets to* MOKRINA.

MASHA. What you standing there like that for? Give me that scarf!

MOKRINA. You can stuff it up your arse.

MASHA *is totally stunned by her rudeness.*

MASHA. What's wrong with you? We gave you our bread back then in the truck, and now you're showing your claws...?

MOKRINA. When I've got food in me, I can bite and scratch, too.

MASHA *wants to rip the scarf off, but* MOKRINA *shoves the pregnant* MASHA *with unexpected force and she falls with a shriek onto the dusty ground.*

MASHA. You fucking bitch, you...

Silence falls on the square like an invisible lid.

MORTKO (*startled*). Whose little minx is that?

RUDENKO. That's Mokrina Staritskaya. Arsei's girl.

MORTKO. I see. Arsei, go and sort the silly cow out, if you want her alive.

ARSEI *walks nervously and with a sense of doom towards* MOKRINA.

MOKRINA. Oh, and who's this coming towards me, if it isn't my darling... Come here, sweetheart...

She runs away from him playfully, all the while getting closer and closer to the tables.

ARSEI. Don't be stupid, Mokrina. Give back the scarf and go home. I'll buy you a hundred scarves like that.

MOKRINA. But I like this one. I won't give it back!!

ARSEI. My love, what are you up to?

MOKRINA *grabs a kebab from the table and teases the* CROWD *with it.*

MOKRINA. Good people. See this meat here – that's what I understand! Look at you all, hanging back like shy young lovers! Don't you deserve a bit of meat?

SAMSON. I've lived on water for two weeks… So what's all this about? Aren't they going to let us sit down?! Run us around –

GOROBETS. Like dogs on a lead.

OLIANA. Promised a feast and we're leaving hungry.

MOKRINA. Help yourselves, there's enough for everybody!

OLIANA. I'll be dead soon, so I might as well fill my belly now.

GOROBETS. I don't care any more.

VOICES. Me neither…

Me neither…

The CROWD *loses its reason and its self-control and rushes for the table without paying any attention to the shouting by* MORTKO, RUDENKO *or the others.*

MASHA, YURKO, IVAN IVANYCH, YUKHIM *and* ARSEI *all try to push people away from the tables. There is some weak pushing and shoving and confusion. The* CROWD, *like a handful of eels, slither through the barrier and start grabbing anything they can from the tables. Someone climbs on the table, someone else grabs a nice*

piece of meat and hides with it under the table, like a dog.
YUKHIM *pours himself a shot of vodka and drinks it back.*

MORTKO *takes his gun out of its holster. He lifts it into the
air. His* ARMED GUARDS *appear behind him. Everyone
freezes.*

GAVRILO *appears.*

GAVRILO. About that time when I killed those crazed peasants
– Lord, I had a lot of responsibility there. The food belonged
to the Government and it was sent for an official occasion
and they'd have had my hide for that, if I'd not had a proper
welcome for Petrenko. So where did that American go, the
one who didn't arrive? You think I needed that bloodbath
outside the canteen? I didn't need that. But none of the
others would get their hands dirty. Not Arsei, not the actors,
not even that idiot Yukhim. Mortko had to do it all. Without
Mortko, nothing gets done.

I remember when I was a little boy, my mother took me
down to the river... And we went through a wood belonging
to the landlord, we took a shortcut... and on the way I
wanted the toilet, because my mother had just fed me soup
and I sat down under a bush and went and suddenly up rides
the landlord on his horse holding a whip and says: 'Are you
making your mess in my wood?' and brings the whip down
right across my back. I was so scared I hardly ever went out
after that. Why did I tell you that? Oh yes... So you'd have
pity on me, Lord. Nobody apart from my mother ever took
pity on me... But she died young, worn out with slaving for
the landlord. So forgive me, God, for all my sins, if you
exist, that is. Although, to be honest, I doubt it. But I'm
praying anyway, just in case, because death will come soon
and take me, too. I'll die at the hands of a traitor. And who
knows what awaits me then...

MORTKO *and his* GUARDS *lower their guns.*

Most of the CROWD *fall down, dead (including*
GOROBETS). *A few scatter at a run (including* OLIANA

and MOKRINA). *The* AGITATORS *and the* ACTIVISTS *run into the truck. Only* SAMSON *is left, sitting at the table. He holds his stomach.*

SAMSON. Oh-oh-oh… Stomach ache… Better to be shot down than die from overeating. Kill me too, Mortko, put me out of my misery.

MORTKO. You can sit and suffer.

MORTKO *sits down at the next table. He pours himself a glass of vodka. He drinks. He takes a bite.*

GAVRILO *sits by him and eats too.*

Where did you come from? That's the second time we've locked you in the grain store. Did you walk through the walls? What are you muttering? Get out of it!

GAVRILO *gets up obediently and walks back through the wall of the grain store, or so it seems to the drunken* MORTKO.

MORTKO *pours himself another drink and drinks it.*

ARTYUKH *arrives with his cart. He sighs, looking round at the work to be done. Then he diligently collects up the corpses.*

Where are you going? Take those shirts off them first! They belong to the State!

ARTYUKH *squares his shoulders and looks proudly at* MORTKO.

ARTYUKH. I'm not your miserable, shit-scraping slave. I'm doing my job.

He carries on doing his job. He goes over to SAMSON, *who is sitting quietly now, and touches him. He is dead. He works out how to get the corpse into the cart – considers one approach, then another. At last he brings the cart up to the table and puts a board between the cart and the table. He humps* SAMSON *onto the board and ties him to it with a*

*rope. Then he goes down underneath to lift the board up. But
it doesn't work. Then he gets up onto his cart and sits on the
other end of the board to lever it up, like a see-saw. But he
doesn't weigh enough to counterbalance* SAMSON. *Then he
throws a few corpses onto the other end, and finally the
board rises, with* SAMSON *on it. All that is left is to push
him down.*

MORTKO *follows all of this with interest.*

May 1933

The Staritskii's house. ARSEI *is digging a hole in the middle of
the kitchen floor to bury a sack of grain.* OLIANA *and*
MOKRINA *are eating some sort of broth.* MOKRINA *is not
quite as emaciated as in the previous scene. She looks more like
a human being.*

OLIANA (*without sincerity*). May the good Lord reward you,
son, for saving Mokrina and me from an untimely death.
Good health to you and all those close to you, boy.

MOKRINA. Where was he before now? When my sisters and
brothers were still alive? When my father... I can't stand the
sight of you. I hate you.

OLIANA *angrily threatens her daughter with her spoon.*
ARSEI *continues digging.*

ARSEI. I'll bring bones tomorrow.

MOKRINA. Don't come here. We'd be better off starving to
death.

MOKRINA *carries on eating greedily.* OLIANA *hits*
MOKRINA *on the head with her spoon.*

OLIANA. Don't listen to her. She's just flirting with you.
Weren't you two courting once upon a time?

ARSEI. When we were children. Over now.

MOKRINA. What are you digging for, that's what I don't understand. Mortko will come and take it all anyway. When he sees we're still alive.

ARSEI. I'll dig the hole deep.

OLIANA. But we won't be able to dig it back out.

ARSEI. What am I for? Call me and ask.

MOKRINA. Perhaps he's digging everyone a hole. So then he can come back with Mortko and be sure of finding it. Earn himself his twenty-five-per-cent cut. Clever boy, Arsei! Is that what's going on?

ARSEI. That's it.

OLIANA. Good thing you didn't marry her. Just look at her – skin and bones. And she used to be such a pretty thing! But she's grown into a stray dog. Our Gafiika, now, when she grows up, we'll give her to you in marriage. You're an important man, these days.

She suddenly chokes. She has a long and agonising fit of coughing. ARSEI *and* MOKRINA *look at each other.*

(*Worn out with the coughing, in a pitiful voice, as if she had only that moment realised.*) My little Gafiika is dead. She gave up the fight first. And here's me eating away…

OLIANA *begins wailing quietly.*

MOKRINA (*angrily*). Mam, you've gone mad. It's always the same, as soon as they have too much to eat, they start pitying themselves. Just don't let them eat too much.

The door is suddenly thrown open. MORTKO *and* YUKHIM *stand on the threshold.* OLIANA *and* MOKRINA *freeze in horror.* MORTKO *surveys the scene triumphantly.*

OLIANA (*quietly, to herself*). The dog didn't bark. (*Remembering.*) Oh, we ate it last autumn.

MORTKO. Enjoy your dinner, good people. I can see the fat cheeks on you Staritskiis from here. Although you swore to me that you'd given everything up to the State.

OLIANA. We had, Mortko, everything, down to the last grain.

MORTKO. So what are you digging a hole for? Your own coffins?

OLIANA. It's all that Pechoritsa's fault. We never asked him. He brought it himself. He brought it and is burying it himself. Hiding it away for himself.

MOKRINA. Mama, be quiet!

MORTKO goes over to ARSEI and looks him in the eye. ARSEI looks down.

MORTKO (*in a quietly fervent voice*). Do you realise what you've done? Do you know who you're helping? You, born a pauper, and you're helping the kulaks?! Do you know how much they hid from us? Do you know how old Feodosii resisted us? We took three carts of produce out of here. Oh, Arsei, I kept on hoping that you'd come round... I thought of you as a brother-in-arms. But I had my doubts back then, when you wouldn't shoot on the square. What have you got to say?

ARSEI. Guilty.

MORTKO. The shame of it! May you drop down into this hole with the shame of it! The court will decide your fate, traitor. And you turned up here with such glowing references. The perfect student, class aware, a hatred of kulaks running in your blood. But what do you go and do? I saw the spark of treason in your eyes all along. There's no place in the party for those who help the class enemy, the saboteur of bread production.

He looks into the hole.

You dug it in deep. Get it out.

ARSEI *obediently gets into the hole.*

(*To* YUKHIM.) And you look through that pile of earth.

YUKHIM *obeys.* OLIANA *meanwhile remembers where she is and starts stuffing the last of the food into herself.* MOKRINA *follows her actions with dull indifference. Then she too 'comes round', grabs her bowl and begins eating.* MORTKO *also realises and tears the bowl out of* MOKRINA*'s hands. Its contents spill on the floor. At this moment,* ARSEI *climbs out of the hole with the sack and the spade.* MOKRINA *stretches out her hand for the sack. But* ARSEI *doesn't give it to her.*

OLIANA (*in a whining voice, to* MORTKO). You're killing us… We'd survived… At least leave that with us…

MORTKO. I'll kill the lot of you.

MORTKO *reaches into his pocket.*

ARSEI *throws the grain sack to* MOKRINA.

ARSEI *puts the candle out.*

8 May 1933

The light goes up. The reading hall. RUDENKO *enters, holding a local newspaper,* Poltava Udarnik.

RUDENKO (*reading aloud*). 'In memory of our faithful and beloved Comrade Mortko who met his untimely death at the hands of the class enemy.

Comrade Mortko was born into a family of paupers in Borshchi, Kiev Region, in 1904. He laboured on a farm from his earliest childhood. He greeted the revolution with joy. In 1924, he joined the Lenin Komsomol and was active in the role of secretary in a local party cell. He organised an army of local political workers and was active in many political campaigns. Between 1927 and 1931, he saw action in Kazakhstan, and was severely wounded by an enemy of the people. Upon recovery, he was sent to Poltava where he was elected Head of the Savinskii Agricultural District. He carried out his work diligently, like a true Bolshevik, oppressing the kulaks and their agents. He became a casualty of the battle for bread on the evening of the third of May, when he died at the hand of the counter-revolutionary Arsei Pechoritsa, a traitor masquerading as a friend of the Soviet Government.

As we remember our comrade and pay our last respects to him, we give our word that the work of the party, for which he died, will be carried out to its conclusion, and we will unite in the struggle against self-seeking Capitalism.'

The voice of RUDENKO *trembles in righteous rage and sorrow.*

8 May 1933

A spring sun. Timid birdsong.

Along the fence lie PEOPLE. *Some are dead, some alive. But the live and the dead can hardly be distinguished. All of their bellies are distended with starvation.*

(This scene could be painted on a backdrop, like in an old-fashioned opera – but with people and corpses painted on, too.)

Living PEOPLE *occasionally walk past. And then, unexpectedly, a sleek-looking, well-dressed* WOMAN *with a baby comes past.*

The radio speaker on the square coughs into voice.

A strange harmony: death, spring and technical progress.

The radio speaker begins playing cheerful music.

ARSEI *stands by* MOKRINA *with his head hanging low.*

ARSEI. Will you pray for me, Mokrina?

MOKRINA. I don't believe in God any more, Arsei. I believe in the Soviet Government. It can do more.

ARSEI. True.

MOKRINA. But still I don't understand anything. Do you, perhaps? You studied in town. You were such an important man. Can you answer my questions?

ARSEI. I didn't learn enough – as you can see. (*He is silent.*) Mokrina, sweetheart, do you remember those jam dumplings your mother used to make? For a long while now the thought of them keeps coming into my head.

MOKRINA. I remember how we used to walk on the lake… in winter. The ice froze, the snow was up to our knees, but we made it across somehow… You carried me back in your arms, because I was wet through and exhausted.

And then I got home, frozen like a puppy, drenched, and my mother scolded me and it was warm in the hut, the wood crackled in the stove and it smelt of borshch and bread and veal, and I felt so happy… That was happiness… Shame. I can't cry, or I'd be crying…

ARSEI. Our love has the taste of those jam dumplings to me.

The AGITATORS *appear on their cart. The same banners, the same cart, the same* AGITATORS…

Who do they think they're going to stir into action? There isn't anyone left.

AGITATORS (*calling for action*).
    Give up your grain for the good,
    The good of the country, you should,
    Be glad to give up your children, your wife,
    And even your life.

    That wealthy Ukrainian denizen,
    Is hardly a Soviet citizen,
    Hides in his cellar, the cheat,
    A half-pound of dog meat.

    From Mr Kulak we'll snatch up,
    All that his family can scratch up,
    Worms, weeds, bugs –
    Real grub.

The radio speaker explodes into a mad Ukrainian gopak (a dance). The AGITATORS *dance.*

The CORPSES, *and those who are dying of starvation, rise and begin their last dance. The* PEOPLE *lying along the fences rise and begin dancing – a whirling jig, a chechetka, a gopak, and something else, all combined.*

There is a thundering of bones. MOKRINA *calls to* ARSEI *who is departing.*

MOKRINA. Where are you going? Don't leave me! You're my husband, remember? We were married. Registered as man and wife.

ARSEI. What sort of husband am I? Don't be silly. We should have been married in the church. Ours didn't count.

MOKRINA. Yes, it did.

ARSEI. Surely you don't still love me?

MOKRINA. Love? All I feel is fear. Can't you see, I've become an animal. I'm afraid that if you go, there won't be anyone to bring me food. (*Stubbornly.*) You are my husband, my man... you are bound to me.

ARSEI. Find someone else. I'm a class enemy. They'll hunt me down and when they find me, they'll torture me.

MOKRINA. Where are you going?

ARSEI. To hang myself.

MOKRINA. Wait...

ARSEI stops. They look into each other's eyes.

Wait... Have you any crumbs left in your pockets...

ARSEI turns out his pockets. Nothing. He shakes his head.

The dance finishes as abruptly as it began. Everyone falls into a large pit, several of the AGITATORS with them, and ARSEI too. Two GRAVEDIGGERS with spades stand nearby.

GRAVEDIGGER (*calling to ARSEI, not without sympathy*). Close your eyes. I'm filling it in.

They begin throwing the thick black earth on the DANCERS.

The OLD WOMAN with an empty bucket crosses MOKRINA's path.

OLD WOMAN. Who were you talking to, Mokrina? Go home, child... You don't look well...

LYONECHKA *limps along towards the administration building. He wears a greatcoat, slightly too large for him. He has a bright, just gaze, beyond his years. He goes over to* MOKRINA *to ask her something, but changes his mind at the last minute and walks past and on to the administration building.*

6 August 1933

MOKRINA *lies on a bench in the hut, her belly distended. From the window a red sunset can be seen. Her sister* GAFIIKA *goes in to see her and sits on the bench opposite.*

MOKRINA (*without fear*). Gafiika, little one... I thought you were dead...

GAFIIKA *gives a pretty, silvery laugh.*

GAFIIKA. Silly! Dead yourself! What a thing to say! I had something to ask you, Mokrina – when you get married, how many children are you going to have?

MOKRINA. Four. Two of each.

GAFIIKA. Well, I want eleven, like our mam. Just think what a big family we'd have, what with the kids and the grandchildren.

MOKRINA. It'd be good.

ONIS'KO *enters. Whilst he speaks the other* BROTHERS *and* SISTERS *move in. They are smiling, handsome. They sit, grinning, on the benches.*

ONIS'KO. Can I join you girls? Am I disturbing you?

GAFIIKA. Only if you don't laugh at us.

ONIS'KO. Laugh? Why?

GAFIIKA. I asked Mokrina how many children she wanted.

ONIS'KO *laughs*.

ONIS'KO. Honestly. You're still kids, you two!

GAFIIKA. I'm just saying. Just think what a big table our dad
would need to build so all of us and all our children and
grandchildren would fit round it.

ONIS'KO. There isn't a table that big!

TODOS. How many people would that be? You can't even
count it!

ULIANA. You'll be at school soon and they'll teach you to
count and read.

TODOS. I don't want to go to school. I want to go and work on
a collective farm.

IAKHIM. Well, you're an idiot. Just listen to him!

ULIANA. Well, I'm going to tell our dad – and he'll give you
your collective farm – and a Five-Year Plan and a kick in the
bottom.

MOKRINA. Brothers, sisters… my own brothers and sisters…
Tell me you weren't buried under the cherry trees? What a
fool I am. What a terrible dream I had!

She laughs and cries.

GAFIIKA. Mam's coming. Come on, you lot! Let's all hide
from her!

*They hide in different places. Some in the stove, some under
the stove, some jump out of the window. There is no one left.
OLIANA enters. She takes MOKRINA by the legs and
drags her to the door across the floor, hurting MOKRINA.*

MOKRINA (*quietly*). Don't take me out, Mam. I'm still alive.

*But OLIANA doesn't hear her. She drags MOKRINA out
onto the street where ARTYUKH is waiting with his cart.*

Mam? Can't you hear me?

OLIANA *stops. She looks dimly at* MOKRINA. *Then she leaves her lying on the threshold.*

OLIANA (*to* ARTYUKH). Come back tomorrow. Still life in her.

ARTYUKH. I'll be back tomorrow, then.

He leaves with his cart.

MOKRINA. How good it is, Mam. I can't tell the real world from my dreams. That's how it should be. How full of joy starving is. Leave me, Mam. My guests are here.

MOKRINA *tumbles into a deep, black pit.*

16 August 1933

MOKRINA *opens her eyes. She is riding on the* AGITATORS' *cart. A skinny nag hobbles along a poor road, dragging the cart.* YURKO *holds the reins. He is small, skinny, black with the sun and the dust.* MOKRINA *opens her fist. On her palm is a piece of soft bread. She puts it in her mouth and chews.*

MOKRINA. Yurko, is that you?

YURKO. It is.

MOKRINA. Where's Ivan Ivanych?

YURKO. Eaten by a cannibal.

MOKRINA. And where are Masha and Vasilii?

YURKO. Vasilii starved. Masha died in childbirth. Hup! Zirka! Fucking horse can hardly put one foot in front of the other…

MOKRINA. And my mother?

YURKO (*thinks, lies*). Weeding the vegetable patch.

MOKRINA. Rubbish, we haven't planted anything for two years. It would be better to tell me right now, while I can't feel anything.

YURKO. With the rest of them.

They ride along in silence for a little while. YURKO *whips the horse but it doesn't react.*

MOKRINA. So how come you're still alive?

YURKO (*brushing off the question*). Doesn't get me. How I am.

MOKRINA. And why am I not with them?

YURKO. I was driving past and Artyukh was putting you into the pit. But you moved your hand to brush away the flies. So I brought you with me.

MOKRINA. What do you want me for?

YURKO. You can sing to me. I like your singing.

MOKRINA. Where are we? What is this country here? No people, no birds, just long grass everywhere. Perhaps I am dead, after all, and you're just teasing me.

YURKO. You're not dead. But aren't you full of questions! This is the Soviet Ukraine. Sing us something cheerful.

MOKRINA *quietly begins singing – a cheerful song. The song becomes louder and more joyful, a whole choir of* YOUNG GIRLS *joining in.*

MOKRINA (*singing*).
A farmer sows a field of corn,
'Poppies,' says the farmer's wife,
'So be it, dear, for who shall care:
A sea of corn or poppies slight.'

A fisherman brings home a fish,
'Crab,' says the fisher's wife,
'So be it, dear, for who shall care:
Wriggling fish or crab that bites.'

A man gives his wife a bonnet,
'A net,' says his wife in hope,
'So be it, dear, for who shall care:
The prettiest bonnet or a net of rope.'

A hunter catches a blue-feathered jay,
'Woodpecker,' says the hunter's wife,
'So be it, dear, for who shall care:
Woodpecker or jay, with blue so bright.'

A man brings home a pair of trousers,
'A tailcoat,' says his wife at home,
'So be it, dear, for who shall care:
Tailcoat, trousers, what I wear?'

* * *

VOICE. Evening, Lord.

Hear my prayer. Everything is fine. It's a sin to come complaining to you. Still, there are one or two things:

Listen, yesterday I was at the doctor, and he discovered a lump on my body. He sent me for tests, but I've come running to You first. Lord, give me a sign. Help me make the right decision. You know how scared I am of operations.

Help my daughter, Ira, find a husband, and help Misha, my son, get a divorce from that bitch. Rid my grandson, Samson, of his asthma and help him at his job interview.

Protect my shop from tax inspectors.

Forgive me for having lots of bad thoughts today about my husband, Andrei. Lord, forgive me for wishing he would die. Save him from his alcoholism, if You can.

I couldn't.

Let my mum live longer, who lost her health on the fields of the collective farms and survived famine and German occupation.

Give peace to the soul of my brother, Sergei, who died after working at the Chernobyl Nuclear Plant.

Give peace to the soul of my dad's brother, Kolia, who disappeared in the Gulag; and the soul of my father, Yurii, killed in the Great Patriotic War.

Give peace also to the souls of my dead aunts and uncles: Khrasina, Sekleta, Iakim, Bronya, Fiodora, Mina, Iavdokha, Todos, Iugina, Gorpina, Iavdokha, Teklia, Safon, Onis'ko, Prokop, Stasia, Khranka, Tofilia, Ianik, Fanas, Gafiika –

Who all died of hunger in 1933.

I hope You don't mind that I've hung their photos over the kitchen table?

There's a lot I don't understand these days.

Forgive me if I sometimes don't speak correctly.

Forgive me if I'm not praying as I should.

Thank you, God, for everything You've given me.

Lord, please help me lose weight in time for my birthday.

The End.

Modern International Plays in Translation
from Nick Hern Books

Marcos Barbosa
ALMOST NOTHING & AT THE TABLE

Lukas Bärfuss
THE SEXUAL NEUROSES OF OUR PARENTS

Evelyne de la Chenelière
STRAWBERRIES IN JANUARY

Olivier Choinière
BLISS

Jean Cocteau
LES PARENTS TERRIBLES

Mikhail and Vyacheslav Durnenkov
THE DRUNKS

Ulises Rodríguez Febles
THE CONCERT

David Gieselmann
MR KOLPERT

Ludmila Petrushevskaya
CINZANO & SMIRNOVA'S BIRTHDAY

Klaus Pohl
WAITING ROOM GERMANY

The Presnyakov Brothers
PLAYING THE VICTIM
TERRORISM

Roland Schimmelpfennig
PUSH UP

Vassily Sigarev
BLACK MILK
LADYBIRD
PLASTICINE

Other Titles from Nick Hern Books

Liz Lochhead
BLOOD AND ICE
DRACULA *after* Bram Stoker
EDUCATING AGNES ('The School for Wives') *after* Molière
GOOD THINGS
MEDEA *after* Euripides
MISERYGUTS & TARTUFFE *after* Molière
PERFECT DAYS
THEBANS

Owen McCafferty
ANTIGONE *after* Sophocles
CLOSING TIME
DAYS OF WINE AND ROSES *after* JP Miller
MOJO MICKYBO
SCENES FROM THE BIG PICTURE
SHOOT THE CROW

Conor McPherson
DUBLIN CAROL
McPHERSON: FOUR PLAYS
McPHERSON PLAYS: TWO
PORT AUTHORITY
THE SEAFARER
SHINING CITY
THE WEIR

Enda Walsh
BEDBOUND & MISTERMAN
DELIRIUM
DISCO PIGS & SUCKING DUBLIN
THE NEW ELECTRIC BALLROOM
THE SMALL THINGS
THE WALWORTH FARCE

Steve Waters
THE CONTINGENCY PLAN
FAST LABOUR
THE UNTHINKABLE
WORLD MUSIC

A Nick Hern Book

The Grain Store was first published in Great Britain in 2009 as a paperback original by Nick Hern Books Limited, 14 Larden Road, London W3 7ST, in association with the Royal Shakespeare Company

The Grain Store copyright © 2009 Natal'ia Vorozhbit
Translation from the Russian copyright © 2009 Sasha Dugdale

Natal'ia Vorozhbit and Sasha Dugdale have asserted their right to be identified respectively as the author and translator of this work

Cover image: Tunji Kasim and Samantha Young; photograph by Julia Fullerton-Batten
Cover typography by RSC Graphic Design
Cover design by Ned Hoste, 2H

Typeset by Nick Hern Books, London
Printed in Great Britain by CPI Bookmarque, Croydon, Surrey

A CIP catalogue record for this book is available from the British Library

ISBN 978 1 84842 045 8

CAUTION   All rights whatsoever in this play are strictly reserved. Requests to reproduce the text in whole or in part should be addressed to the publisher.

Amateur Performing Rights   Applications for performance by amateurs, including readings and excerpts, should be addressed to the Performing Rights Manager, Nick Hern Books, 14 Larden Road, London W3 7ST, *tel* +44 (0)20 8749 4953, *fax* +44 (0)20 8735 0250, *e-mail* info@nickhernbooks.demon.co.uk, except as follows:

Australia: Dominie Drama, 8 Cross Street, Brookvale 2100, *fax* (2) 9905 5209, *e-mail* dominie@dominie.com.au

New Zealand: Play Bureau, PO Box 420, New Plymouth, *fax* (6) 753 2150, *e-mail* play.bureau.nz@xtra.co.nz

South Africa: DALRO (pty) Ltd, PO Box 31627, 2017 Braamfontein, *tel* (11) 489 5065, *fax* (11) 403 9094, *e-mail* Wim.Vorster@dalro.co.za

Elsewhere: Casarotto Ramsay and Associates Ltd, see details below

Professional Performing Rights   Applications for performance by professionals in any medium and in any language throughout the world should be addressed to Casarotto Ramsay and Associates Ltd, Waverley House, 7-12 Noel Street, London W1F 8GQ, *fax* +44 (0)20 7287 9128, *e-mail* agents@casarotto.co.uk

No performance of any kind may be given unless a licence has been obtained. Applications should be made before rehearsals begin. Publication of this play does not necessarily indicate its availability for amateur performance.

Mixed Sources
Product group from well-managed forests and other controlled sources
www.fsc.org Cert no. TT-COC-002227
© 1996 Forest Stewardship Council
FSC